S0-DUW-190

May 2015

COACH

The Life
of
Charlie Lee

Delaine —
  When I think of my
wonderful years as a Toy,
I think of you! Always
have, always will.
  Thanks for the memories!

Love,
Ralphene

COACH: The Life of Charlie Lee
Copyright© 2014 by Ralphene Lee
All rights reserved.

For additional copies or information,
contact the author at ralphene@aol.com.

Design and page layout by Kristy DeVaney.
Printing by Sir Speedy Printing, Roseville, California.

First Edition, First Printing
ISBN: 978-0-692-34028-8

On the Cover: *Charlie being congratulated by colleague Larry Fletcher as his wrestlers lift him in celebration after winning the 1973 Northeast Sub-Section Tournament.*

Charlie's official photo for the 1961 Hula Bowl.

On the Back Cover: *Charlie and Ralphene at the Power House outside Ennis, Montana, August, 1997.*

The Lee Family: David, Susie, Ralphene, and Charlie at David's house in Daly City, California, 2010.

Dedication

This book is dedicated to the "Special Three"—Alex, Matt, and Sam, as we referred to our grandkids.

Charlie's grandkids meant more to him than anything in the world especially in his later years. The stories in this book illustrate how their grandfather was raised and the positive influence he had on others throughout his life.

—Ralphene Lee

Gramps and the Special Three talking about the "Klop Egg" and its magical powers in 1998.

Sam, Matt, and Alex at Alex's Master's Graduation Ceremony at Southern Utah University in 2013.

Foreword

This book is composed mostly of memories written as emails by Charlie Lee. The first were written in 2004 while we were living in Maryland for part of the year to be near our grandkids. Charlie's good friend Targe Lindsay, principal of Bella Vista from 1975-1983, suggested that since he had a very successful teaching and coaching career, he should put some of his experiences in writing. Charlie was reluctant at first, but as he was urged on, he found more subjects to write about. This writing became a source of enjoyment which he continued until his death in 2010. This book would never have been possible without Targe's ongoing support and encouragement.

Charlie was a wonderful husband, father, and grandfather. However, the stories recorded here are not about experiences with his children or his grandchildren. Those stories would fill a large book. This collection focuses mostly on Charlie's coaching career and younger years. Charlie's thoughts have not been changed, but I have taken the liberty of adding a few memorable moments I felt should be included. Each anecdote is written by Charlie, unless otherwise indicated.

This entire project was a labor of love for me. Recalling these moments made me once again appreciate the wonderful and unique man I was married to for almost 50 years.

—Ralphene Lee
Carmichael, CA
January 2015

Charlie and Ralphene watching BV wrestlers.

Targe Lindsay with Charlie's grandkids—Sam, Matt, and Alex—in his workshop in 2012, helping them make a gift for Susie. What a special bond—being able to collaborate with their mother's high school principal and their grandfather's dear friend.

Sam presenting Susie with the results of her work during the summer of 2012 when Alex, Matt, and Sam lived together on campus at Stanford.

Table of Contents

Table of Contents

Table of Contents

Table of Contents

A Coach's Son
By David Lee

Not many kids get to grow up as the son of a wrestling coach. It is an honor and a privilege with which I have been blessed. My earliest wrestling memories are of sleeping under the scoring table during that first BV Invitational. I remember looking up at the clock on the BV gym wall, 12:30 am, and guys were still wrestling hard on all of the mats. I remember sitting in the corner coaching chair with my dad when Vic Henderson wrestled Fred Bohna in the finals of the 1974 California State Championships. I attended the next 10 California state tournaments.

A couple years later, driving to the state tournament held 10 minutes from our house, my dad said, "Keep an eye on this Dave Schultz kid, he just returned from competing in Russia against their best freestylers." That same tournament I bet the kid sitting next to me (Marty) a dollar on the 120-lb. finals match, Casey Noland vs Marty's brother, Jackson Kistler. I went to all the tournaments. My mom even started taking me to Dad's practices as early as first grade. From that early age, I could tell that my dad's wrestlers respected and trusted him. They would give their all for him every time. The room was small and the concrete walls would sweat during the

Charlie, three-year-old Susie, and six-month-old David practicing wrestling moves in Grandma Lee's kitchen.

Four-year-old David at a tournament with his dad and BV wrestlers Julian Salazar and Jim Mackin.

cold winter practices. It wasn't long before the Sacramento Super Stars were using that same small wrestling room to hone the skills of what would become one of the best kids' clubs in the country.

My dad had a unique style of coaching, one that I feel he picked up from his Iowa football coach, Forest Evashevski. His style was less about teaching technique and more about instilling a belief in yourself and a desire to always give your best effort. I always joked that the only move he taught was what he called the heavyweight roll. That, and using super 8 technique films of Wayne Wells shown on the wrestling room wall. A lot of his early teams won on sheer guts and toughness. By the time the Super Stars occupied the high school ranks, we had the experience and technique to go with the discipline and toughness. My four years at BV we went 2nd, 3rd, 2nd, and 2nd in the state tournament.

This book is for everyone who wrestled for my dad, and for all of the friends and coaches he met along the way.

Charlie and David on the awards stand at the 1984 California State Wrestling Tournament. David had just been presented an award for becoming California's first three-time state champion.

Born a Bronco
By Susie Lee Stadnik

I grew up playing underneath the bleachers of the Bella Vista gym, rode to tournaments in the back of our pickup truck with the wrestlers, and have always been my brother's number-one fan. Many nights when we were little, my dad would come home and say, "Suz, get in referee's position. I want to show David a new move." It was a foregone conclusion that I would attend Bella Vista—I was born a Bronco.

My dad always supported me in my sports—softball, volleyball, basketball, and track. It was hard to be a Lee and not be competitive. And he knew just the right way to get under my skin to get me to work harder. After dinner we would go out to the front yard to play catch so I could work on my arm. He would tell me, "You throw like a girl," and that would make me fire the ball even harder. Thanks to many hours of practice in our front yard, I am proud to say I DO throw like a girl!

Susie at age two...always a BV fan.

My freshman year at BV, the girls' teams had to practice in what was then called the "Girls' Gym." The boys got to practice in the "Boys' Gym," which was much larger and nicer. Title IX was passed five years earlier, but it clearly hadn't made its way to Bella Vista. My friends and I led the charge to change that. You have to love the fact that Coach Lee's daughter pushed to get the gyms called the Big Gym and the Little Gym and to get equal practice and game time for the girls' and boys' teams (which of course meant less time in the "Boys' Gym" for the boys' teams). I'm sure my dad took a lot of ribbing for that, but I also know that he was proud of me for standing up for my beliefs—although he always called it the Boys' Gym around me!

Bella Vista's girls' volleyball team at the first-ever state volleyball tournament in 1978.

I have many memories from growing up attending all of David's and my dad's teams' matches. Two are permanently seared in my mind. One was when David won the World Schoolboy Championship in San Diego when he was 13 and I was 16. I remember watching the American flag being raised as they played the National Anthem with David standing on top of the podium. The other was when David was in the finals of the California State Tournament in 1982. As all who know the story are aware, he spent 45 long seconds on his back, only to come back and win what was the first of three state titles. I spent that entire match screaming and yelling like only a sister can.

Contrast that to my dad who remained calm and collected, as always, in the coach's corner.

Susie and David after David's first California State Wrestling Title in 1982.

I grew up in the wrestling world as "David Lee's sister" and came to Bella Vista as "Coach Lee's daughter." Not many people can lay claim to two such notable titles, and I was proud of both. Fortunately, I was able to forge my own path while attending the school where my dad taught. David started as a freshman my senior year at BV, and he started as a freshman my senior year at Stanford. I recently attended several wrestling functions and without even thinking, introduced myself as David Lee's sister!

SUSIE LEE, Bella Vista — Hit .387, called "a stable force and very disciplined" by Coach Carol James, has 4.0 GPA, will attend Stanford.

Photo from Sacramento Bee *All-Metro Girls' Softball Team. Susie received the Gordon King Award for Outstanding Student Athlete at Bella Vista in 1981.*

Letter from Coach Marc Sprague

September 16, 2010

Dear Ralphene and the Lee Family,

The passing of your beloved Husband, Father and Grandfather brings much sorrow to us all, but also brings moments of joy as we all reflect back on Charlie's life and how he affected us individually.

I so remember his quiet demeanor at mat side as he worked his kids with the touch of a masters hand and directed his kids as a conductor directs the symphony to create a masterpiece for all to see and appreciate.

Charlie taught me that calmness and silence can speak louder than words and can effect our performance in a profound positive way. I will carry with me this great life's lesson as one of the most profound learning experiences of my coaching career. I call it the Coach Lee effect.

In much sorrow,

Marc & Alfie

1635 NW WHITMAN ST. · Camas, WA 98607 · (503) 956-7022 · www.CobraWrestlingSystems.com

Charlie and Marc Sprague were two of a kind. They each shared a passion for the sport of wrestling and were instrumental in building character in young athletes. Marc's Cobra Wrestling Club in Portland, Oregon, and Charlie's Bella Vista teams sometimes trained together and exchanged home wrestling trips. Marc remains active today, providing wonderful opportunities for young athletes in the Portland area.

We Are Family
By Nancy Schultz

We all like to say we are part of the "wrestling family" and for me I think that feeling began when I met the Lee family. Charlie Lee, the patriarch, led his family and the "family of wrestling" with kindness, knowledge, integrity, and love. Dave Schultz and Dave Lee were the best of friends for many years. They were like brothers, and Dave Schultz leaned on the Lee family for guidance and support in many ways.

At the height of his career and international success, it was from Charlie Lee that he took advice for his strategy and game plan for some of his toughest matches. It was from Charlie Lee that Dave drew his clues of successful balance of wrestling and family life. It was from the entire Lee family that our family found a special place in the wrestling world. Thanks, Charlie! We all miss you.

Nancy Schultz with Charlie and Ralphene at Charlie's induction into the California Wrestling Hall of Fame in 2001.

Introduction

Coach
By Sheldon Marr

I had been "grappling" with ideas for a title for this book since I began the project. Many were discussed; none seemed appropriate. Finally, I told Susie I thought I would just call it "Coach." Neither of us could think of anything better, but the decision was not firm. A few days later, Sheldon Marr sent the following piece to be included in the book. Once I read it, I was sure we had the right title!! Thanks, Shel!

—Ralphene

Charlie with Sheldon Marr at the 1998 Jujitsu America Hall of Fame Ceremony where Shel received the "Instructor of the Year Award."

Coach Lee was my coach, my mentor, my friend, and one of my heroes. I wrestled under Coach for three years to a record of 75-12, but didn't get to wrestle my senior year due to a broken neck in a pre-season scrimmage. The following year (my first year of college), three schools in the Sacramento area needed a wrestling coach, and all called Coach Lee for a recommendation. To my surprise, Coach gave all three my name and phone number! I chose Highlands High School which was 0-12 in the league the previous year. My first year there, we were 5-7, and my second year we were 7-5. I know that's not like winning state, but it made me want to be a coach myself, which was something I never really thought about until Coach's recommendations. From there I became a PE major with plans to be a PE teacher and wrestling coach!

My senior year of college I returned to judo competition and was invited to live at the Olympic Training Center in Colorado and train for the 1984 Olympic Team. After leaving the OTC, I took a job in the Denver area as wrestling coach at Cherry Creek High School and finally earned the name "Coach" myself. After that, I opened up the Grappler's Edge Academy (now known as Edge MMA & Fitness).

I've now been involved in the martial arts for 50 years and wrestling for 40, and have been somewhat successful at both as an athlete and as a coach. But what makes me so proud to be called "Coach" today is not that my wrestling team won state, or that my grappling team won 18 national titles, or that I coached the U.S. Grappling Team to 6 world team titles...

What makes me so proud to be called Coach, is because of one great man who I had the privilege of knowing and learning from—a man who we never called "Charlie" or even "Mr. Lee," a man who we all called and affectionately knew only as "COACH!"

1976 Bella Vista Wrestling Team

Introduction

Sacramento Bee Article by Joe Davidson
September 14, 2010

Hometown Report
JOE DAVIDSON

jdavidson@sacbee.com

BV's Lee coached until end

Charlie Lee was a multi-sport star at San Juan High School.

Even when his body started to fail him, Charlie Lee coached. Even when he could barely speak, the man mentored.

He would do it from his living-room floor, with scores of Bella Vista High School wrestlers stopping by during recent years for instruction and video critiques. When Parkinson's disease made speaking difficult, Lee would tap a teenager on the shoulder and nod. An approving smile spoke volumes. Lee was a coach to the end.

Lee, a California Wrestling Hall of Famer who steered one of the best prep dynasties in area history, died Friday of a heart attack. He was 71.

"Charlie was amazing, my hero, for how he dealt with his illness," said Lee's wife of 49 years, Ralphene. "When Parkinson's made it too difficult to hunt or fish – and that really hurt him – we would go to lunch or to the dog park. To Charlie, it was still doing something he enjoyed. He never complained. I don't know how any of us could suffer like that and not complain."

Patience and understanding were Lee virtues. He was a composed coach in a sport full of frantic leaders who explode off their seat amid chaos at the corner of a mat.

Lee presided over the Broncos for 22 seasons, retiring after the 1983-84 season with a crowning moment. Son David became the first California wrestler to capture three successive state championships, winning his last 118 matches.

Bella Vista went 248-28-1 under coach Lee, including a stretch from 1979 to 1984 when the Broncos won five Sac-Joaquin Section championships and finished second in the state three times and third twice.

DAVIDSON | Page C6

FROM PAGE C1

David, who won a national championship at Wisconsin in 1989, works in commercial real estate in the Bay Area. His sister Susie Lee Stadnik, a three-sport star at Bella Vista who attended Stanford, is a director of technology for a school in Maryland.

A multi-sport star at San Juan in the 1950s, Lee was a starting tackle in 1958 for the Iowa Hawkeyes, named national champion by the Football Writers Association of America. Lee met Ralphene in college, and she traveled with him as he capped his 1960 senior season in the All-American Bowl, the Copper Bowl and the Hula Bowl. Their marriage included black and gold wear – Hawkeyes colors – and the bowl games made for a whirlwind honeymoon.

Lee attended the Houston Oilers' training camp in 1961, a setting that included Billy Cannon and George Blanda.

"He was in camp for 10 days, called me and said, 'This isn't for me,'" Ralphene said. "Charlie said he wanted to teach and coach, and he sure did."

For information about services for Lee, contact Ralphene at Ralphene@aol.com.

WRESTLING

Wrestling
By Ralphene

Bella Vista's rise to state and nation-wide prominence in the sport of wrestling was exciting. Not having wrestled in high school or college, Charlie knew very little about the sport until he went to Central Missouri State College to work on his master's degree, and became best friends with Lefty McIntyre, the wrestling coach.

Charlie's first year at Bella Vista was the 1962-1963 school year. His wrestling team that year won the first varsity championship earned by the school in any sport. That championship was followed by many others, and the creation of the Sacramento Super Stars in 1977 contributed greatly to Bella Vista's future success in the sport of wrestling.

This club was Charlie's idea and was formed because of a developing interest in kid wrestling in the area. The club was open to young boys who were not yet in high school. An ad was placed in the *Sacramento Bee*, tryouts were held, and the original group was limited to 20 because of the size of the Bella Vista wrestling room. Throughout the years, various coaches worked with the group. Charlie was not the practice-room coach, although he did coach the kids at matside whenever he was free. A national championship was the goal of each wrestler, and many boys achieved this goal. The quality of the group is evidenced by the fact that in August of 1979, four Super Stars were on the 25-member United States World Schoolboy Wrestling Team that competed at the World Schoolboy Tournament held in San Diego, California. Never before had four boys from the same team been a part of this elite group.

Although many of the young wrestlers went on to BV, many went to various other high schools in the area. However, Charlie kept his eye on "his wrestlers" throughout their wrestling careers, no matter what high school they wrestled for. At high school tournaments he would frequently call a young wrestler from another school aside and give him pointers on his technique—even though in a future round he might be facing a BV wrestler in his weight class.

Charlie was known for seeking the toughest competition for his teams, and his high school coaching record was 245-28-1. His teams finished second three times, third twice, and fifth once in a state that has over 700 wrestling teams eligible to compete in one huge state tournament.

Charlie with Tracy Yeates, David Lee, Cody Olson, Ken Gaudreau, Casey Noland, and Mike Lee at the 2001 California Hall of Fame induction.

Best of all, the friendships formed during Charlie's coaching career will last throughout the years. Thanks to all those athletes, BV students, coaches, teachers, and parents who were a part of Coach Lee's life.

The Lee family at one of David's collegiate tournaments in 1985.

Wrestling Program

I have been asked many times over the years why the BV wrestling program was so successful. I'm not sure this would be the blueprint for all wrestling programs, but it worked for BV. Most of the things that follow can be controlled by the coach, but not all.

When I took the job as wrestling coach, I was fortunate to have the support of the football coach. Getting the football players out for wrestling is important. All my assistant wrestling coaches were top-notch, but I was lucky to have two outstanding ones. One was Bruce Summers, whose overall knowledge was outstanding for the jv level. He was a real fire-and-brimstone kind of coach who in his own way really excited the kids and attracted a lot of kids to him. My personality was somewhat different.

1979 Sacramento Super Stars Youth Wrestling Team

The other was Roy Erickson, who knew absolutely nothing about wrestling, but was one smart cookie, and what he lacked in wrestling knowledge, he more than made up for in enthusiasm. Wrestling knowledge is not the most important thing in a jv coach. These two men were super-enthusiastic and had terrific personalities, and they kept most all of the kids out for the program. That is the real key. When you are trying to build a wrestling program, it is essential to have numbers. Of course you don't always have the luxury of picking your assistants at the high school level, but if you do, look for those qualities.

Hope to get a principal who supports the wrestling program. My second principal was a dream to work for. He was very supportive of all athletics and pretty much kept a "hands-off" policy. He allowed me to keep all the money we raised from our yearly wrestling tournament and use it to support the high school team. I could order whatever the program needed most to help us be successful.

The Spring Invitational Wrestling Tournament was a HUGE success. At one point it was the very best kids' tournament in the USA. It got our high school wrestling program a lot of attention. We usually cleared between $11,000-$13,000 a year from it. And you better believe that money helped the high school program. This tournament met its demise for a couple of reasons. After I retired from coaching, the new coach did not have the contacts we had amassed over the years. Also, insurance became a real factor.

At the time, San Juan Unified School District had wrestling in the 7th and 8th grades. If you are to have any success at all, you must have a feeder program. I was most fortunate that Carnegie Middle School had Sebastian Adorno. He was a super-enthusiastic coach and would routinely have over 100 kids out for wrestling. No need to say how important that would be for the high school program. If your school does not have a feeder program, see that it gets one. It is absolutely essential. Then it almost goes without saying that as a coach, you are constantly recruiting among the student body. I tried talking to EVERY SINGLE KID in school who I thought might come out for the team. You have to be on top of the kids academically; don't lose a kid because he is doing poorly in school. INSIST every kid make weight. I had only one kid in 22 years not make weight. This is extremely important. Many a match is lost by a kid not making weight. Each coach to his own method, but get that point across.

Of course if you want to reach the top rung of high school wrestling, you will have to start a club. That is a whole book in itself (another time). If you aspire to that, you had better be single or find a wife like mine (and they are RARE).

Take care of the small points and be organized in practice (that means writing on paper what you want to do every practice—most coaches do not do this). Keep the mat clean and sterilized every day—every single day—make sure you have a good manager, make sure you always dress out in wrestling gear for practice, keep up with new techniques, be sure you scout all your opponents, schedule the right competition, make sure the team has top-notch equipment, put out a printed program to give the kids recognition—something they can be proud of—travel in the summer, constantly make sure kids don't quit, keep your assistants on the ball, have enough money on hand—this is all part of having things fall into place. And finally, find a way to get your wrestlers to do many of the hard things they do (attending every practice, making weight, running on their own, conducting themselves in a manner that would make you proud) because they do not want to disappoint you. This is a tough one.

And now for the final secret for a kid to become a good wrestler. Give this some thought and follow through on it and see if I am not right on: NEVER MISS PRACTICE!

BV Spring Invitational

BV hosted the first freestyle wrestling tournament in Sacramento in the spring of 1971. I wanted to raise some money for the program and thought this would be a good way. It was TOO GOOD. That first year we had more than 1,100 wrestlers and even though we kept things moving, we did not finish until 1 am. Part of the reason was, of course, that the "bad point system" was in use at that time. Everyone was guaranteed at least two matches.

The next year we took a bold chance. We sort of made our own rules (much to the chagrin of the United States Wrestling Federation). We ran a line-bracket tournament using freestyle rules and said you must lose to a finalist to be able to wrestle back.

I designed a special double-eagle medal which was far nicer than anything else being given at that time. We made the tournament pre-registration and limited it to the first 500 wrestlers who signed up. (No more 1 am matches!) There were a lot of kid wrestling clubs around.

In the first few years we had 8-and-under, 10-and-under, 12-and-under, 14-and-under, 16-and-under, and open divisions. We made up our own weight divisions each year, based on the previous year's turnout (much to the consternation of the USWF). We did not require a USWF card and no one had to show proof of their insurance. The district said its insurance covered everything, because it was a school-sponsored event. I quickly accepted that and moved on, because insurance became a huge stumbling block later on. In our third year, I decided to drop the open division (which we had kept in order to have enough refs to officiate the whole tourney) because our numbers grew so large.

We soon realized that the tournament was on the verge of becoming something special. We began awarding gold statues of the famous Greek Wrestlers, mounted on walnut bases with a gold plaque on the base that read "Bella Vista Invitational Champion." (The story of how those awards came about would be another interesting read—maybe someday.)

Because of all our travels with David and the Super Stars, we had made a lot of contacts with wrestling people throughout the U.S. We pulled out all the stops, and I got in touch with our friends in Southern California, Oregon, Montana, Wyoming, Arizona, Idaho, Nevada, and Colorado, and convinced them to come to the "best" age-group wrestling tournament in the country. I took a chance that year (kind of like saying my mother says it's okay if your mother says it's okay) because not all of those teams had said they would come. It was pre-registration only, and in order for your wrestler to be ceded, you had to send in all the ceding information ahead of time. I did all the ceding and drew up all the brackets. I guess I was a pretty good salesman, because USA Oregon brought down about 30 studs, Roy Pittman from Portland brought two buses full of kids, Jim Gressley from Tucson, Arizona brought kids, Lanny Bryant from Montana brought his club's better wrestlers, as did a club from the Reno area, and a host of strong clubs came from Southern California. My big selling point was that this tournament was to be hosted by the Sacramento Super Stars who had just won their third national title, and all those coaches knew it. Marc Sprague of USA Oregon was the first guy I called. I jokingly told him if he thought he had a wrestler or two who could handle this competition, to "come on down." That was all it took. When Pittman heard Sprague was coming, he brought his whole club. Now we had a TOURNAMENT!

Charlie and Ralphene at the head table of an early BV Spring Invitational.

Once these coaches saw the level of competition and those gold trophies, the word spread, and over the next five or six years we had the best and strongest age-group tournament in the nation. As far as I know, it was the only pre-registration age-group tournament around.

Some things the coaches liked: programs with all the names bracketed, the cedes listed, complete history, and place winners of all previous tournaments—FREE. This program contained more wrestling information than could be read over a very long breakfast. Free admission for coaches at the door. $1 admission for spectators. A big bonus was that competitors could weigh in the night before. Many people had never heard of such a thing at that time, but 99% of the coaches, kids, and parents loved it. We still had a morning weigh-in, but since most of the wrestlers came from so far away, they always came the day before, and those early weigh-ins really appealed to them.

We never had less than 500 kids, and though I had said "limited to the first 500 wrestlers" I never turned a kid away, so sometimes we had close to 600, but no one ever complained. In our strongest year, we had all the Super Stars wrestle, and the above-named clubs and states brought kids. Throughout the years, we also had individuals from New Jersey, Ohio, Oklahoma, and an All-Star

Age-Group team from Japan. The Japanese team took home one trophy. The coach said ours was absolutely the toughest tournament he had ever seen. That made us all feel pretty good!

Ours was the only wrestling tournament I ever saw, other than the Olympics, that started absolutely on time. I don't mean two minutes late, I mean exactly on time. That became something of a trademark. Old-timers at breakfast would tell first-timers, if they had a kid up early, they had better be ready on time! Ralphene gets the credit here. She ran the head table with a veteran group including Cindy Noland, Roseanne Yeates, Margot Berry, Cheryl Petersen, Don Orton, and Tom Boustead. I manned the mic and assigned mats and called the matches. I was also the one-man protest committee. (I could count on one hand the number of protests we had throughout all those years.)

After that first tournament, the Sacramento Area Wrestling Association (SAWA) was formed. John Phillips, Bill Flake, John Horillo, and I were the group who started it. We set up a small schedule, maybe five tournaments that year. I was voted president, probably due to the success of our first tournament. Things were off and running. Bella Vista remained the only tournament that used the unique pre-registration format with freestyle rules and collegiate bracketing. We also did not require any association card or proof of insurance. As years went by, we ran into trouble with the national association for not abiding by their weight divisions and not requiring a card or insurance. I was just lucky. We had started the first post-season wrestling tournament. I had a principal, Targe Lindsay, who did not breathe down my neck. So I kept all the proceeds in an off-campus account. We used the money for the high school team, and later for the Super Stars. When asked about the insurance, I always said the district had insurance coverage, since it was held on district grounds, and that is what I had been told. I don't think we could have afforded the premium the national association would have wanted.

At any rate, that's a little history of how freestyle tournaments got started in the Sacramento area.

The Famous Statue

David and John Loomis became friends when David was about six years old. David took up the sport of judo, at which John excelled, and John took up wrestling. John was like a member of our family from that point on, going on family vacations, practically living at our house.

Anyway, for David's birthday—maybe age seven or eight, I don't remember, John presented him with a small plaster of Paris version of the famous marble statue called "The Wrestlers." Mrs. Loomis was into ceramics and had found the statue while pursuing her hobby. We all thought it was such a very cool gift!

Ralphene and I got to thinking about that statue. At that time the BV Spring Invitational was growing by leaps and bounds. I would say it was the "Ironman Tournament of the West Coast" for that day and age. It was an age-group through high school tournament, so we would have as many as 32 weight classes. There would often be four or five western regional champions in the same weight class. The competition was fierce. People came from all over the western U.S. As it grew in prominence, we were constantly seeking to upgrade our awards—we wanted them to be unusual and distinctive. Slick-looking red flannel-lined jackets with Bella Vista Spring Tournament Champion on the back, stuff like that.

I came up with the idea of using that statue in some way. The white plaster statues only cost $2 each. So we experimented a bit, and with the help of several parents, we came up with what we felt was a first-class award.

The only place to get the statues was in Los Angeles. We tried having them shipped, and they invariably arrived chipped, arms broken off, etc. So Mr. Loomis would drive his battered old pickup to LA each year and pick up a supply of statues to use. He was a woodworker, and he came up with a nice walnut base. Clint Tichenor would spray them metallic gold for us. It was truly a group project. And the final product cost about $7 each!

Famous statue of "The Wrestlers." Handmade by Super Star parents as the championship award for the BV tournament.

Well, once the kids saw those statues, you can imagine how the word spread. Roy Pittman used to bring a whole school bus full of his kids' club wrestlers down from Portland, Oregon. They would sleep in the gym the night before. They usually took home three or four statues—they were a tough club.

We would take a break before the finals and bring out a couple cafeteria tables with the statues on them. Quite an impressive display! We practically needed armed guards to keep the spectators away! We always had cool awards for second through fourth too, but nothing rivaled those statues.

By Plane, Train, and Automobile

I always felt that taking the kids out of the area to wrestle was a good thing. The problem was cost. That was one of the main reasons for starting the BV tournament—to raise travel money.

We were successful at that; we usually cleared at least six or seven thousand dollars after all expenses, which was really great, considering the quality tournament it was. I wanted to spend most of the money on the kids whose parents had worked to put on the tournament.

The first "out of town" trip we took was by car. I arranged to wrestle two duals and a tournament in Palm Springs. Coach Bruce

Summers's parents lived there, and we had an absolutely fantastic dinner together.

I don't recall how we did in the wrestling, but the wrestlers had a great time. They got to see some neat sights around Palm Springs. We also went to Disneyland. GREAT TRIP! Worth the money! The following year's tournament was a huge financial success, so our next trip was by plane. We went to Oahu, Hawaii. The basketball team joined us. We wrestled two duals (won both) and everyone had a great time.

Again, another successful tournament and another trip, up we go to Portland, Oregon on Amtrak. Most of the wrestlers had not ridden on a train, so this was a neat experience for the kids. We wrestled in the Benson Polytech Tournament. A terrific tournament. I think we took second. (I just asked Ralphene but she couldn't remember either.) I do remember that David in his freshman year lost in the finals to a senior who had a scholarship to Oregon for the next year.

Those were the three big trips we took. Of course we would always go to Clovis or Santa Cruz or Susanville or Herlong. I liked to get out of town!

1973 team preparing to board a flight for a wrestling trip to Honolulu, Hawaii.

The Highest Tribute
An email written by Ralphene
to Targe Lindsay in 2004

Targe,

I don't know if I have ever shared this with you. I consider it the highest tribute to Charlie's coaching ability that ever could be. As you know, Dave Schultz was like family to us, really from David's high school years on. He came up and visited my class at Trajan School, let the kids wear his Olympic medal, etc. Wrote a letter (in his lovely manuscript printing) that was three or four long pages, answering every question my kids had asked of him. (I still have that letter. Made a copy for each kid in my class.) Mark came up too. I think he came on his own at a different time, but I still remember him in Room 8. The kids asked him to take off his shirt and show his muscles, and he did! Boy, I was impressed, and I'd seen a lot of muscles by then.

Anyway, during a certain window of time, about two or three times a year, the phone would ring. It would be Dave, calling to talk to Charlie. He usually called him Charlie, in that drawl of his that I can still hear, while most people called him Coach. After visiting a while, Dave would get to the point of his call. He would say that he had such and such an opponent coming up at the U.S. Open, World Trials, or whatever competition. The opponent was quite frequently Kenny Monday, but there were several others. And he would say something like, "OK, Charlie. What's my game plan?"

The world's most famous and talented wrestler, with the entire USA wrestling coaching staff, plus many more, at his disposal, and he calls Charlie to talk strategy concerning his toughest opponent. Now that I recall it, it just blows me away. I guess I didn't think that much about it at the time. If that doesn't speak to Charlie's coaching ability, nothing does. Just had to share that with you. Perhaps you'd heard it before, but never from Charlie. That is a certainty. And thanks again for being my sounding board. You have forever been Charlie's biggest fan. I know that.

—Ralphene

Dave Lee and Dave Schultz in Newtown Square, Pennsylvania in 1991.

Ralphene and Dave Schultz before leaving with the U.S. team to Barcelona for the 1992 Olympics. Ralphene was Official Pairing Master for the U.S. team, and Dave was a U.S. team coach.

Dave Lee, Dave Schultz, and Coach Chris Horpel on a rare break during a workout in the Stanford wrestling room in 1985.

Dave Lee is congratulated by Wisconsin Assistant Coach Dave Schultz after defeating Baron Blakely of Oklahoma by a score of 14-6 in the 1989 NCAA Finals, March 18, 1989, The Myriad, Oklahoma City.

May-June 1977 Cover of
The Young Wrestler Magazine

The May-June1977 issue of The Young Wrestler, *featuring Dave Schultz on the cover as a high school senior. He had competed for the United States in the Tbilisi Tournament in Soviet Georgia and earned a silver medal—the highest-placing American at the tournament. Dave followed this up by winning a California state high school title, wrestling two weight classes above his normal division. Later that same year he won the U.S. National Open Greco-Roman Championships and the award for most falls in the least amount of time.*

July-August 1977 Cover of
The Young Wrestler Magazine

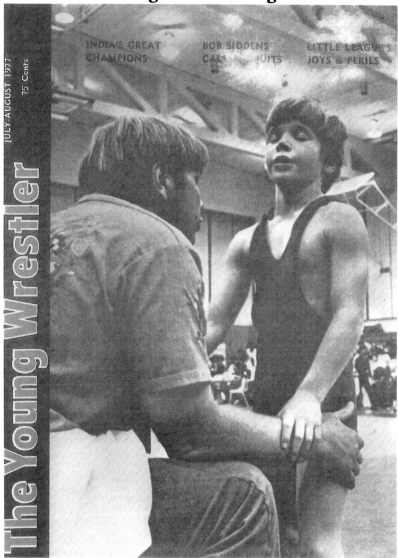

JULY-AUGUST 1977

75 Cents

The Young Wrestler

INDIA'S GREAT CHAMPIONS

BOB SIDDENS CALLS 'EM JUITS

LITTLE LEAGUE'S JOYS & PERILS

This picture of Charlie and David, taken at the Western Nationals in 1977 when David was eleven, was on the cover of the July-August issue of The Young Wrestler. *The photo was taken by David's sister, Susie. The picture exemplifies the relationship between father and son, coach and wrestler.*

Quick Thoughts

In 22 years of coaching, I only had one kid miss making weight.

I had a kid in a PE class who was willing to be a non-suit every day. He would just take an "F" because he did not want to participate in any of our units. So I made a deal with him. If he would suit up, he could stay in the towel room (we still had towels at that time) all period and come out when the next class came in. If he did that, I would give him a "C" on his report card. OK! He thought that was great. But he had to be there every day and dress out. Lucky for me, after about a week he decided to dress out and take part in the regular class.

Once I used an X-acto knife from the art department to lance a carbuncle on Larry Vasquez's neck because the doctor said he couldn't wrestle with it. Lucky again.

I did the same thing for one of Gordon's basketball players. The kid was standing on a desk so I could get a better look at the knee (it was just behind the right knee). Gordon was kind of balancing him. When I cut into the thing, the kid passed out. Before Gordon or I could catch him, he hit the floor. He was ok. Lucky me, lucky Gordon!

During a badminton unit I had gotten the big cherry picker from the janitor and had a kid get in the basket, and while some other kids moved him around, he would get the birdies off the ceiling beams. I told them to be careful and not go too fast, because I didn't bother to put the safety bars out. These kids were freshmen and didn't always do as they were told. I wandered out in the lobby, and when I heard a bunch of laughter, I go back in the gym just in time to see the cherry picker crash to the floor with this kid still in it. The kids who I told to be careful had started to race the thing around the gym, and it had toppled over. The kid was not hurt. Lucky me!

Mrs. Connelly (Casey Noland's mother-in-law) had two sons who wrestled for me the same year. In an effort to pocket the $5 their mom gave them for haircuts, they had me cut their hair. I gave them my standard military cut. Mrs. Connelly was hopping mad. I mean HOPPING, because the family was going to have their family portrait taken at a studio that evening.

At the Western Nationals in Bozeman, Montana, Bruce Summers loses to Marc Sprague by one point in the finals. Howard Bair gets into a big argument with Bill Flake and moves Howie from Placer High School to Bella Vista to wrestle. Wow!

Mr. Olson comes to me at the BV Spring Tournament and asks if I would be interested in having Cody wrestle for me the next year. I say, sure, but you must be squeaky legal with the residence, etc. because people will find out. Mr. Olson's reply was, "Consider it done!" What an addition that was!

Earl Hicks stays home the day of a big match because he was not feeling well and wanted to be ready for the match that night. The principal found out and told me he couldn't wrestle. We lost the match by four points, one of our 28 losses over the years.

When Casey Noland had to forfeit at the San Juan match, we lost by three points, the second of BV's 28 losses. The tie against San Juan came at BV when Richard Cotham pushed a kid who threw an elbow at him, that the ref later claimed he did not see. He penalized him one point and that made his match a tie and also made the team-score a tie.

When Tom Beimel used to coast in practice, I would have him work with David. When David would slack off, I would have him go with Cody. Cody never slacked off! Cody and David were good for each other. Their drilling was more fun to watch than most matches.

California Bound

After finishing one full year at Central Missouri State College in Warrensburg, Missouri, I received my master's degree in education. It had been quite a year: the football scandal, the firing of coaches, the interview with President Truman. Ralphene had signed a one-year contract with the elementary school on Whiteman Air Force Base. Full salary $2,300 a year, take it or leave it. We were so poor, I would hustle the high school kids at the local pool hall in eight-ball for a dime a game.

I had written my old high school principal, George White, asking for a recommendation for a football job at Elk Grove High School. Much to my surprise, he offered me a job at Bella Vista. A personal interview was mandatory, so I was fortunate that he was going back East to visit his daughter. He interviewed me at our apartment in Warrensburg, and I was given a job as full-time PE teacher, plus assistant varsity football coach ($180) and head varsity wrestling coach ($180). My take-home pay was $333 a month. We rented a fully-furnished little cottage right across the street from my parents for $80 a month. I thought if I ever took home $500 a month, we would be in hog heaven. A thousand dollars a month take home was just a pipe dream at that time.

More Memories

I remember a match at Encina. There were a few bad calls, and the crowd was getting vocal. Finally, the ref threatened to forfeit the match if the crowd made any more outbursts. Roy Erickson told me he was all set to throw a penny on the floor, which, since we were at Encina, meant we would get the forfeit! Fortunately, it did not come to that.

I also remember a dual meet against Encina at Bella Vista for the league championship. Bob Towers was the referee. It was an exciting dual that came down to the heavyweight match. Kim Lolo, our heavyweight, won by a fall, and we won the match by one point. Our kids were so excited they ran onto the mat to congratulate Lolo. The fans were yelling like crazy. And speaking of crazy, here comes Frank Berry from about the 8th row of the bleachers and lands right in the middle of the mat. This was too much for poor Bob Towers, and he penalized BV one point for unsportsmanlike conduct, which meant the match was now tied. I thought Frank was going to hit him, he was so mad, because his landing on the mat right out of the blue is what caused Towers to award the penalty point. After a couple of meetings with George White and the powers that be, we had the point taken back and we won the championship.

Wrestling   30

My Reply to Targe's Questions

Coaches I most wanted to beat: Crowl, Cavallaro, Flake. In no particular order.

That first year we just wrestled ten duals, plus several tournaments. In making out the schedule, several coaches I talked with told me how tough Roseville was, and that they didn't think it was wise to wrestle them twice. Young and too confident, I went ahead and set up a home and home. John Lucena was the coach at that time, and he talked me into home weigh-ins. I heard later that he was not always on the up-and-up on those weigh-ins. I doubt that was true. I think it was just sour grapes.

Roseville beat us real good the first match at their place. Remember now, we had a pretty darn good team. When they came to our place, I insisted that both teams weigh in at BV. Most all of his kids were over weight, so he just bumped everyone up a weight. I liked our chances now. They beat us as bad as the first time! I should have heeded those coaches' advice. One good thing did come out of those losses. I learned the value of scouting my opponent ahead of time. Roseville did certain things (moves) that, had I known about them, I could have better prepared my kids for. I did not make that mistake twice! They were the better team, and better coached at that time.

Best fans. That's a tough one. We really had some super fans. They seem to get better when you win. Put the "Popcorn Gang" at the top of the list! Bob Hager, Don Orton, and Tom Boustead. They don't come any better. They never missed a match or a tournament. Knew all the kids, sat together at the top of the bleachers eating their popcorn and yelling their heads off. When a BV wrestler had his opponent on his back, you could hear Boustead yell from the top of the bleachers, "Pin the Dude!!"

And of course, the Cadells. Nel and Ernie were BIG Bella Vista wrestling fans. They came to our matches, even followed David to the NCAA tournament when he was in college. They would invite us up to their lovely place in the country for parties. Ernie was a Stanford grad who played pro ball for the Detroit Lions. He was also the area's largest Chevy dealer. The Cadells had a swimming pool in their back yard in the shape of a chevron. When you rang the doorbell, it played, "See the USA in your Chevrolet." When asked once why the Cadells were so interested in BV wrestling, since they had no connections to the school, my answer was simple: "Ernie just likes to back a winner!"

Run-ins: can only recall a few. I'm sure there were more, but these I remember. I had a kid by the name of Bob Bennett, a heavyweight. I didn't start him in a certain match, and that made his mother mad. She cornered me after the match and proceeded to tell me what a poor coach I was, and that I would never go further than BV. (She was right about one thing.)

Jim Mackin was a freshman at the time. He was a scrappy kid with lots of heart and some real promise. We were wrestling San Juan and their 103-pounder, a kid named Phipps, was going to pin our guy. So I put Jim in to avoid the pin and save three points. Phipps proceeds to throw Mackin all over the mat, really worked him over. I had told Jimmy to expect that, but if he did not get pinned, it would be just like a win. Jim fought his heart out, but got pinned with just a few seconds to go in the match. When he sat down I told him what a great job he had done, and that I was very proud of his performance. His dad felt otherwise. He raked me up one side and down the other. I guess from his point of view, I deserved it. Jim did go on and wrestle for four years and was a league and sub-section champion.

Never did get tired of practice. I think had we not been so good year in and year out, and if I had had to put up with losing and all that comes with it, I might have lost interest.

Assistant coaches—I hope I don't forget any. Bruce Summers, Roy Erickson, John Mahoney, Jon Abernathy, Ron Blankenship, Barry Alan.

Various Wrestling Trips

In 1977, Mike Salazar made the World University Greco-Roman Wrestling team for 18-21 year olds. Quite an accomplishment! The tournament was held in Las Vegas, and Barry Rannells and I decided to go. (Ralphene wasn't sure what the real reason was.) We had a great time. Mike won a couple matches, but did not place. Barry was on a red-hot streak and could not lose at poker! He very generously picked up the tab for the entire trip.

Talk about a small world—when David was 21, he made a trip to Japan with his roommate, Erik Duus. Erik's dad was head of the Asian Studies Department at Stanford, and his mom was Japan's foremost author. Her most famous book was *Tokyo Rose*. They lived part-time in Japan and part-time in Palo Alto. While in Japan, the boys went to a very small Japanese village to visit with a judo friend of Erik's. David was shown a scrapbook of the Japanese University team competing in world competition. The book fell open, and David found himself looking at a picture of his dad watching Mike Salazar wrestle a young Japanese boy. What a shock for David!

In 1970 I decided I wanted to see the World Championships. They were being held in Edmonton, Canada. Barry and Roy decided to come along. Barry and I wanted to do some fishing, so we left ten days ahead of Roy, who we were to pick up in Idaho Falls. Barry's friend Glenda was staying with her mother on their 8,000-acre ranch just out of Burney. We arrived just in time for a great dinner. The next morning, after another great meal, Glenda's mother asked if we would mind giving the hired hand some help setting some sprinkler pipe. We said we would be more than happy to. Little did we know that we were to pay dearly for those great meals. I was wearing my fishing waders and it must have been 90 degrees.

It was back-breaking work, and it took about five hours. Now it was time for lunch. I was so pooped, I could hardly lift my fork. Mrs. Gardner asked if we would mind helping stack some hay bales in the barn. What could we say? This was worse than the sprinkler pipe. We had planned to stay for three or four days and fish nearby Hat Creek. I told Barry I could not take another day like that. He seconded the motion, and he made up some excuse, and we were off for Montana early the next morning.

We were having breakfast one morning, and this guy tells us about this great fishing spot that is about a two-hour drive from where we are. A place called Henry's Fork on the Snake River. Off we go. The fishing is fantastic! We rented a raft and float-fished the Box Canyon. We stayed there and fished the Harriman Property, the Railroad Ranch area. All of this probably doesn't mean much to you unless you are a true fly fisherman. This area is now considered the Valhalla of fly fishing in America. We fished it just before it was "discovered." The day before we left, we were fishing at Last Chance, and there were signs advertising riverside lots for sale for $400 each. Barry said, "Let's buy a couple." We had the cash on us, but just never got around to it. Now there are no more lots to be had, and I hear that lots, not even riverside, go for $300,000 and up.

We drove about 100 miles to Ennis, Montana. That was the start of our annual trip to the Madison River. We had excellent fishing during the day. At night we played five-card stud poker in the back room of the Silver Dollar Bar. It was no limit, but the pots never got too big. We played there three nights; I can't remember if we won or lost. But that's not what I remember it for (more on that later).

Now it's time to get Roy, so we drive to Idaho Falls and pick him up. We stop to fish the Madison again on the way back. The fishing is great once again. It's the start of the salmon fly hatch, and Roy catches the biggest trout I ever saw caught on the Madison. It was at least five pounds.

We again hit the stud game in Ennis. Poor Roy, he loses $50 and is inconsolable. He wants to go back to Idaho Falls, says he can never afford the trip now. We persuade him to go on. Next stop—Twin Bridges, Montana. We are fishing for brook trout on a small mountain. On leaving the stream, I run over a rock and bend my drive shaft. We are really a long way from anywhere, and it is getting dark. As luck would have it, along comes this cowboy in his battered pickup, and gives us a ride to town. Barry and Roy stay at the local bar and grill where they have the cook fix all the brook trout, which they consume. In time the cowboy agrees to pull my car to town, about 15 miles, for a fifth of Jim Beam. Agreed.

I get back several hours later, all the fish eaten and the grill closed. I had to have a tow truck come from Missoula and tow the car to a Ford dealership, where they had to make a new drive shaft.

But I was so lucky. I got ahold of an insurance agent who said running into that rock was an act of God, so my insurance covered everything, even a car rental for the five days it took to make the new drive shaft.

On our way to Edmonton we stopped for a couple days and took in the Calgary Stampede. Everyone should experience that once in their life. We made it to Edmonton, and I watched the entire tournament. I got to see the great Alexander Medved, three-time Olympic and twelve-time World Heavyweight Champion. That made the trip for me. I write the whole trip off on my income tax and get audited by the IRS (another story). I win my case!

The Interview

At a Bella Vista basketball game, Larry Fletcher and I were running the clock and keeping the book. There was a reporter from one of the local radio stations seated right behind us who was taking notes using a tape recorder. At halftime he got up to go to the snack bar, and he left his tape recorder at his seat.

Larry thought he would have some fun (can you believe that?) so he takes the recorder and says he is this reporter and he is interviewing Charlie Lee, Bella Vista's wrestling coach. We talk about Bill Flake at Placer and Joe Cavallaro at Del Campo. I say some outrageous things about them, (can't remember now just what) then he asks how come BV has such a good wrestling program. I tell him that one of the things that really helps is that our principal, Targe Lindsay, has allowed us to set special rules for outstanding wrestling prospects to circumvent the attendance rules. In addition, each kid is given his own tutor and allowed one date a week with the cheerleader of his choice. All varsity wrestlers eat free in the cafeteria, and each wrestler receives a bonus for each tournament he wins. I explained it worked on a sliding scale. $50 for regular season tournaments, $100 for league, $200 for sub-sections, $500 for sections and choice of any Chevrolet or Ford car or truck, since Ford and Chevy sponsored our scholarship program.

Well, this guy comes back from the snack bar and resumes recording notes on the game, never noticing what Fletcher has done. When he gets home and starts to go over his notes he hears "the interview." He thinks it's pretty good, so he runs it on the air the next day. At the beginning of the program he explains what it's all about, but I guess this one lady missed that part and only heard the interview. She called the station and was truly irate. She is going to the school board and demand an investigation. She can't believe such things are possible! What kind of coach is this, the principal should be fired, on and on. They finally got things straightened out. Never a dull day!

Potpourri
Again, in response to questions from Targe

As to Don, Gordon, and Larry—all were supportive of the wrestling program. Don would try and convince the football players to wrestle. Larry was always recruiting for me. Gordon always told the good basketball/wrestling freshmen prospects that "if they didn't make the basketball team, they could go out for wrestling." One year there was this big freshman kid who I had in my PE class. Gordon wanted to get him out for basketball, and I wanted him to wrestle. I told him and his parents that I thought he would be a section champion at the very least before he graduated. I think because I had him in PE, I was able to convince him to wrestle. So he came out for wrestling. About a week later, we had a scrimmage with Vacaville HS in our wrestling room. They had a senior heavyweight—a real tough kid. Well, I made the mistake of letting this freshman wrestle the Vacaville kid. The other kid put a whopping on him and hurt his shoulder. The next day the frosh basketball team had a new member. The kid's name will come to me. He ended up being a pretty fair varsity basketball player. Had he stayed with it, he also would have been a very good heavyweight.

It was the custom of the league wrestling coaches and their wives to get together before the season and have dinner at someone's home. It was a chance for everyone to get to know each other, and for the coaches to BS about their teams. I don't know if other sports did that or not. There was never a coach I didn't like (except the

San Juan coach for a period of three years—you know the Casey Noland story). Joe Cavallaro was very excitable and easily set off. Mike Salazar drove him crazy. Bill Flake was probably the best coach of the three. He wanted to beat us in the WORST way, and year in and year out, his teams always had the best chance. After Placer came into our league, they never did beat us.

Jim Enos was kind of in a world of his own. He always ate lunch in the locker room, didn't socialize much with the rest of us, and baseball was his life. He worked real hard at it. He told some kids that they should concentrate on baseball, and baseball alone, which was at times a sore point with some of us.

Don't recall ever having to "eat my words" or bend the rules slightly to achieve a certain end. I do know that I was often accused of illegal recruiting—i.e. Jack James, the Kitchen boys, Tracy Yeates, Mark Loomis, Cody Olson, Tod Wagner, the Henderson boys. But I never did. They came to us legally.

As to memorable comebacks, the ones I alluded to, Mike Lee and Barry Alan, are pretty much it for the high school wrestling. In the kids' program a few matches really stick out. The first one concerns the Super Stars team, the last two are individuals.

We had taken the Super Stars to Bozeman, Montana for the Western National Junior Wrestling Championships. A feature of the tournament was that each club could pick a ten-man team, and they would score points for the team title. But the kids had to be members of your club. You were not supposed to bring in some ringer. It just so happened that we had brought just ten kids, so that's our team—David Lee, John Loomis, Tracy Yeates, Ken Gaudreau, Tony Kitchen, Sam Tichenor, Tod Wagner, Bruce Summers, Lance Diamond, and Howie Bair. Some team!

There was a club from Las Vegas coached by Jerry Wager who was a FILA ref and a big shot in amateur wrestling circles. You won't find me calling many people a bad name and having Ralphene agree with me, but that's the case here. Nuff said about Jerry Wager. There was this really, really tough kid from San Jose named Armando Gonzales. Wager put him on his team and said he commuted to Las Vegas to work out with his club. HA!!

The tournament committee held a special meeting and did not allow Gonzales to compete for Vegas. The Super Stars won the team title handily.

In 1978, David was wrestling in the finals of the National AAU Championships in Lincoln, Nebraska against a kid named Blake Bonjean, who later wrestled for the University of Minnesota. It was the last period, and David was ahead by a single point. With about fifteen seconds to go, Bonjean shoots in and picks David up completely off the ground and is set to slam him to the mat and win the match. Well, I know it is hard to picture, but as Bonjean takes him to the mat, David puts a standing coop-scoop on Bonjean and pins him. These wrestlers were twelve years old. The crowd was stunned. So was I—so was Bonjean!

Perhaps the greatest American kid wrestler of the time was Marc Sprague from the USA Oregon Wrestling Club. His dad was the coach, and a great one. Their team was the best around, about fifty kids, and Marc was the shining star. He NEVER lost! He dominated people. He was so slick and polished for a kid of fourteen. He was the Oregon Division One State High School Champion as a freshman. This was his last tournament as a kid wrestler. This particular tournament determined who qualified for the World Schoolboy Championships. Marc was wrestling John Loomis in the finals. Everybody in the building was around the mat to watch this match. Sprague usually overwhelmed other wrestlers, but he had a kid here who was pretty tough himself. The match was tight. Sprague was ahead by two when John shot in and picked Sprague up high and took him to the mat as time ran out. In this type of wrestling there is a referee and two mat judges. When the ref awards points, one or both judges have to agree. The referee on the mat was the big AAU mucky muck, the head of all the officials. When Marc hit the mat, the ref signaled a two-point takedown which would have tied the match and forced an overtime, and then signaled one point for high amplitude. When he did that, he made a point of emphatically pointing his finger at the judges as if to say, "I want no disagreement here," and there wasn't any. It was a tremendous win for John. Sprague came back to beat John for the World Team, but that was John's moment.

The Placer Match

My wrestling record at Bella Vista was 242-28-1 over 22 years. Several big matches come to mind, but my all-time favorite was the dual meet against Placer High at BV in 1983.

We had a very good team and had won 72 straight matches. No one wanted to beat us more than Bill Flake, the Placer coach, and the feeling was mutual. I had the match figured on paper—who had to win, who had to pin and not get pinned, etc. I had us winning by 18 points. Should be no problem, right? Wrong! Flake's kids wrestled like Olympians. Ken Gaudreau lost, Danny Tennant lost, Sam Tichenor lost. Before we knew what happened, we're behind 27 to 9. Flake was going crazy, jumping up and down. He turned to Darryl Jones and yelled, "I've got him now!" Then he pointed at me and pumped his fist. I called a time out and got the kids together behind the bench. I said, "Did you see that? Nobody can do that to us in our gym. We have five wrestlers left and we need four pins. Do It Now!" Flake is telling his kids, "Just don't get pinned, and we can't lose."

Tom Beimel goes out at 154 lbs, and pins his kid in 20 seconds. David pins his kid at 165. Now our kids are really juiced. Joe Baker is wrestling a really tough kid. He would be lucky to beat him, let alone pin him, but he is so excited, seven men couldn't hold him down. He pins his man. Next is Jerry Petersen at 190 lbs, another tough kid. Flake is pleading with his kid, "Just don't get pinned." To no avail. Jerry pins him in the first period. The score is 33-27 in our favor.

Now Mike Whiting, our heavyweight, just has to not get pinned, and we win. Mike is wrestling a MUCH better wrestler. I tell him, "Mike, if you ever had a match in you, now is the time to pull it out." Mike was a smart kid and had a big heart. He was on his back maybe ten or twelve times. He would scoot out of bounds, he would fight until the period was up. He did as good a job as anyone ever has for me. We win 33-30! Flake cannot believe it.

As he came across the mat, I was tempted to give my good friend Bill a little fist pump of my own.

1983 Bronco team
Bella Vista 33/Placer 30

Charlie and Bill Flake participating in a chili cook-off.
Charlie and Bill had a friendly rivalry throughout their
many years of coaching. As this picture shows, they were also
very good friends.

The Robes

In my second year at BV I decided it was time for a new look. We were league champions the year before, and the kids, I felt, would like the change.

Robes were a popular item in the Midwest at this time, especially with the college teams, but no one (NO ONE) wore them out here.

I got white satin robes with red trim and red satin ties for the waist. The kids didn't know quite what to think. Some said other wrestlers would laugh at them. I said once you beat your opponent, there would be no more laughs.

The robes were different. Fortunately, we didn't lose many matches, and suddenly the robes looked pretty darn good!

1964-1965 BV Capital Valley Conference Champs

Another Story

I think the year was 1964. The Far Western Wrestling Championships were being held at Alameda Naval Air Station in the Bay Area. It was the Western Zone Qualifier for a chance to go to the Olympic Trials. There was a high school tournament being held at the same time, so I took some of the high school wrestlers down to compete and also have a chance to watch the open wrestlers. I think it was Gene Ernst, Richard Hanson, and Larry Vasquez, but I am not sure. Anyway, the kids talked me into entering the open heavyweight division. The kids thought their old coach was pretty tough. There were only three entrants in the heavyweight class. My first match was against Gary Stensiland from the Multnomah Athletic Club out of Portland. A pin in 20 seconds—guess who got pinned? My second match was with a wrestler from the San Francisco Athletic Club, a real moose, weighing about 320 pounds. Same result. But if anybody asks, I placed third in the Western Zone Wrestling Championships and qualified for a shot at the Olympic Trials. I have a medal to prove it.

Would You Believe It?

It was in the Year of Our Lord, 1962, and I had been teaching at BV for one year. I was the wrestling coach and assistant varsity football coach. Those duties, plus teaching five periods of PE, made it a must to have a good stopwatch. I wanted one that was accurate and reliable and not a nuisance to carry around.

With those requirements in mind, I set out in search of the perfect instrument. What I settled on almost earned me a permanent bed on the couch. We had been married almost two years. I was bringing home $352 a month, and Ralphene was not working because of the impending arrival of "Little Suz," as we called her.

When I walked proudly through the front door and announced that I had finally found a GOOD stopwatch, she said, "That's great! Let's see it." I proceeded to show her my new $525 Rolex watch, which had a stopwatch along with the ability to tell time. My wife does not use bad language, but this act provoked even her to call me a pretty bad name. "How could you do that? Don't you know we can't afford this thing?"

I tried to explain that this was a wonderful instrument, and that it would really help in wrestling. Now I could tell the wrestler how much time was left in the match. Nothing worked. Finally, after a few rough days, Ralphene forgave me and life went on.

I had that watch for about five years. It caused me nothing but trouble, always in for repair. And that was always a $100 bill. One day while driving to work, I heard this guy on the radio tell about this outfit in Texas that was paying cash for old, quality watches. Well, my Rolex fit that bill. The guy said to just send in your watch and tell us how much you think it's worth, and we'll send you a check. RIGHT! Almost every day I heard this ad on the way to work in the morning. So what the heck. I called the number and when this guy answered, I told him I had a Rolex Chronograph I wanted to sell. He asked me what kind of condition it was in and how much I wanted for it. I said it was in great condition and I would take $1,000 for it. He took my name and address and said I would be getting a check for $500 in a week or so, and then I should mail the watch in, and I would get the remaining $500 in another week or so.

A month came and went, and guess what? No $500 check. The ad was still running almost every day now. Ralphene and I laughed a lot over such a scam. Who fell for those things? I said I was going to give them another call, just for the heck of it. This time I told the person I talked with that I wanted $1,700 for the watch. He said I would get the check in a few days. Well, five days later I get a check in the mail for $850. I still thought it a scam. I went to my bank, and they cashed the check and it cleared. So I mailed the company the Rolex and a week later I received the other $850. That's a strange one!

No Hemingway

Did you know I was an author? I want to be accurate on the year, but I am not real sure. I believe it was 1963 or 1964. At that time, wrestling nationally had gone from twelve weight classes to thirteen weights. However, all the wrestling score books allowed for only twelve weights to be recorded without having to turn the page and use the first line of the next twelve-man page.

I was taking a class at Sac State at the time, for a couple units, in order to move up the pay scale. My good friend Gene Schroeder was taking the same class. I was telling him about how I thought a wrestling score book that allowed you to record thirteen weights without having to use the next page would be a sure-fire winner. I said I thought every high school in the country would buy them. So we decided to design one. I provided the ideas, and Gene put them on paper.

Now I find out that in order to sell the thing, we will need an actual finished score book. We do some checking around for a printer, and finally find one that will cut the plates and give us a finished book for $1,000. A lot of money for both of us at that time. We do it. We now have the Lee/Schroeder Wrestling Scorebook. Now how do I market it? The biggest marketer of wrestling score books then was Wilson Sporting Goods. I called them up, and finally get to talk with the right person. I explain what this is all about. He says it sounds interesting, but he would have to see the actual scorebook.

Ralphene and I went back to Iowa every summer. This summer was no exception. When we got there, we relaxed a few days, then drove to Chicago to the headquarters of Wilson Sporting Goods Company. I hunted up the guy who made the decisions on scorebooks, and it turned out he liked the idea. So now I'm an official author. I sign a contract. I'm so excited I don't even know what it says.

I had talked with a printing company in Burlington, Iowa about the cost of printing, shipping, etc. so when the Wilson guy wants to discuss price, I think I'm ready. As it turned out, we paid nineteen cents a copy to have the book printed. Wilson paid us $1.19 plus shipping. So Gene and I split $1 per book.

The first order was for 1,000 copies. We kept our arrangement with Wilson for several years. We made a little money. Eventually better scorebooks came out, and we lost the deal with Wilson. (Wilson sold the book for $2.95.)

Ralphene just read this and she reminded me that this was the time when we were so poor that we had to break a $2 bill my dad had given me years before, that I always carried for good luck, to pay the bridge toll on the way home from Chicago!

Hair Today, Gone Tomorrow

It was in my third year at Bella Vista that I got into the barber trade. That year the wrestling association adopted a hair-length policy. It stated that hair had to be off the ears and a certain length in front, and so on and so forth. The point was that the rule was made, and we had to learn to live with it. It was a pain in the rear. The refs would line up each team before weigh-ins and check the wrestlers' hair. If a boy's hair length did not satisfy them, the wrestler had to cut some off and try again. If it still did not pass, try again. Well, I was having none of that. The first time one of my wrestlers did not pass the hair test, I took the tape scissors to it and never had another kid fail the hair test.

I started to take pride in my haircuts. I bought a kit with scissors and clippers, and after some trial and error, I became quite good. It got to where I was probably giving 20-25 haircuts a week. Had no complaints, since I found out the kids would get $5 from their folks for a haircut and have me cut their hair, and they would pocket the bucks. That is—until I cut the Connelly brothers' hair. Mike and Paul were both wrestlers, so I gave them both my typical wrestler haircut, which meant they would not need another haircut for three months. I did not know this, but their mother had arranged for the family portrait to be taken the next day! When their mom saw those haircuts, those boys were in big trouble!

Things were going along just fine with my haircutting until one day our principal, George White, called me into his office and told me the members of the Fair Oaks Barbers' Union were filing a complaint against me for giving haircuts without a barber's license. I was really hurting their business. I could have fought it, because I was not charging the kids. But I thought it was not worth the headache to fight it, so that was the end of my barber days. Much to the delight of some parents and kids, I would guess.

Go Figure

What would you think of a PE activity that 98 or 99% of the kids just loved, where kids who were daily non-suits suddenly dressed out? Where kids would cut other classes, and some teachers would actually write notes for students to get out of their class to come to ours? Where kids you hadn't seen for days suddenly showed up? Where the level of physical activity was greater for everyone than anything else we could do? And the kids just LOVED it! Where we never had nearly as many injuries as we did in a football, soccer, or even volleyball unit? Where kids hated for class to end? Where some kids did a rain dance and some kids would wear paper sacks over their heads (the unknown comic) so we wouldn't know they had cut class to play another period? Where the level of excitement in the locker room was akin to a football locker room before a big game? And the kids would beg for the coaches to take roll early? Naturally, it was banned.

I used to tell James and Bartley, two of the women PE teachers, that dodgeball embodied everything that made America great. I'm glad they never asked me what those things were. But they were so furious after that first statement, they never bothered to ask.

More Dodgeball

At one time dodgeball was so popular that I thought we might be able to make some $ from it. I organized a tournament and held it in the Boys' Gym (before it became known as the Big Gym, and THAT is another story!). We charged an entry fee and admission at the door. So we made a little money. It was Bella Vista against La Sierra in the finals. Well, things got pretty heated. About that time, I had to leave. I don't remember why. I gave the megaphone to Fletcher. Later I found out that a near riot broke out between the BV parents and the La Sierra parents, and Larry got hit over the head with his own megaphone.

You could make dodgeball a varsity sport, and it would easily outdraw basketball. Plus, you could have 50 or 60 kids on a team. Just think of all the kids who would be involved. A lot of the so-called dirt-baggers would get involved, so you would probably save a lot of kids. The cost would be minimal, and you could use old football scrimmage vests for uniforms. If you used the old-time rules, there would be no holding it back. It certainly is no more violent than football.

The Sand Bags

I was always looking for a way to make conditioning more fun. Upper body strength is essential if you are going to be a successful wrestler. I also wanted to challenge the mental toughness of my wrestlers.

I came up with the idea of using sand bags to accomplish both goals. Each wrestler had his own bag, and they differed in weight, depending on the weight of the wrestler. The whole team would get their sand bags and form a circle around me. On my command they would pick up their bag and hold it with both hands, and move it around, maybe straight out in front or overhead or whatever. The kids would have to mirror my actions. (My bags had no sand in them!) It was a killer drill. Sometimes they would jog around in a circle while using the bags. I often had a kid lead the drill, and we would see who could last the longest. You could get a pretty good idea of who was mentally tough.

Classy Lassie

We had a terrific wrestling team in 1982. I was always looking for ways to keep things fun and keep the guys motivated. Aerobics was not all that popular at that time, but I thought it would be a good way for the wrestlers to build their conditioning.

I got this beautiful, and I do mean beautiful, instructor from my gym to come in for a half hour each day and lead the team in a tough aerobic workout. The kids just ate it up. They did not want to let her show them up. So that was an excellent way to warm up for practice. Channel 10 somehow got wind of it and did a segment on us for their nightly sports report. We were in the news a LOT that year!

Wesley Gaston—One I Miss

The first time I saw Wesley Gaston was when he tried out for the Sacramento Super Stars. He was, I believe, in the seventh grade at Carnegie Middle School. It was no easy task to make the Super Star team. We carried no more than 20 kids, and the competition was stiff!

Everything else being equal, the parents usually were the deciding factor. How willing were they to travel, to make all the practices, to work at the Spring Invitational, to sell advertising space in the program, etc.? This was seldom a problem. Every parent who brought a son to a Super Star tryout knew what was involved.

In Wesley's case, it was a no-brainer. Not only was he a fine wrestler, but his mom, Pat, and dad, Charlie, were all you could hope for in club parents. Charlie was kind of laid back, didn't say too much, but Wesley's mom was something else. You could hear her if you were out in the parking lot, and Wes was in the gym wrestling. Charlie and Pat made every match Wes had as a Super Star. Traveled to Montana, Nebraska, Arizona—no matter, they were always there.

When Wesley came to Bella Vista, he was really the start of the "super kids" who were to make BV so tough for the next six or seven years. Mrs. Gaston just assumed that Wes would make the varsity as a freshman at 95 pounds. And in most cases, he would have. He was probably the second or third-best kid in the Sacramento area at that weight. Unfortunately for Wes, (as his mother saw it) the best kid in the area was Scott Kitchen, BV's 95-pounder.

It was not unnoticed by Mrs. Gaston that Wes would be varsity at any other school. Encina had a particularly good group of light weights from 95 thru 120 pounds. Pat came to me after a practice (Wes practiced with the varsity) and said she just could not see Wesley being on the jv team when he would be a starter on any other team in the area. She was thinking, she said, of moving him to Encina—and I knew she was serious.

Of course I didn't want to lose a kid of his ability. But I said that if she were determined to do that, to go ahead, and I would wish him the best. (But please, Lord, NOT Encina!)

I explained to her that I would not move Kitchen up to 103. So that meant Wes would be jv all year. But I felt that if he stayed, he would be part of a terrific team in the next few years. With Bruce Summers, Tod Wagner, John Loomis, David, Ken Gaudreau, and some other young Super Stars all coming in, he would do really well. She knew all those kids, so she knew what I was talking about.

Well, as they say, the rest is history. Wesley wrestled varsity the next three years, was the best kid at his weight, a section champion, and one of the very best room-wrestlers I ever coached.

Sadly, Wes was killed in a car accident four years after high school. He made a glass etching for me when he graduated from BV. This etching still hangs in our living room. It shows a wrestler doing a cradle, one of his best moves, and says simply, "I'll Remember You." I CERTAINLY WILL.

Footnote by Ralphene

Although Charlie focused on Wesley in this email, Wes had a younger brother, Todd, who also wrestled for the Super Stars and BV. Todd was an easygoing, fun-loving kid who everyone liked to be around. And a heck of a wrestler.

But Todd was so much more than that. In the last few years of Charlie's life, realizing that the two of them shared a deep love of fishing, Todd would take Charlie fishing in his bass boat. They would often leave in the morning while it was still dark, and be gone until after sundown. This was no easy task, as it involved Charlie taking lots of meds, needing assistance walking and getting in and out of the boat, and much more. I can still see Charlie's face when the phone would ring and it would be Todd, calling to arrange a fishing trip. Those fishing trips were a source of so much pleasure for Charlie.

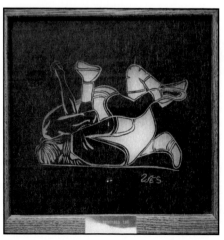

Glass etching done by Wesley Gaston and presented to Coach Lee in 1981. It says "I'll Remember You." (Thank you, Colleen Butler, for all your inspiration to BV students throughout the years.)

Wrestling

The Choir Boys

In 1981, I knew we were going to have some special teams, now that a bunch of the Super Star club kids were going to be together. I wanted to have something uniform-wise that would really make our team stand out. I ordered snow-white warmups, both tops and bottoms, with small red and black stripes running down the sides and a red lining to the hoods that when unzipped laid neatly on the back. They were really stunning, except the mothers hated trying to keep them clean.

1981 Bella Vista Section Champions

That year I was able to get us invited, for the first time, to the Clovis Invitational Tournament. It was the toughest high school tournament in the western states. At the ceding meeting when they got to the 112-pound weight class, I raised my hand and said I thought David should be considered. Dennis DeLiddo, the Clovis coach at the time, said there was no way they were going to cede a freshman. Well, I got into an argument with him, and he said our team looked like a bunch of "choir boys." Well, we had David, Ken Gaudreau, Tracy Yeates, John Loomis, Jack James, and Bruce Summers, all clean-cut and chubby-cheeked. Dressed in those white sweats I guess that they did look like choir boys. DeLiddo and his Clovis team usually won their tournament and had won the last couple of California state tournaments as well. They had never heard of Bella Vista and never dreamed what they were about to run into. We won five weight classes, taking home five of those handsome Stetsons the champions were always awarded (including David, as a freshman). We broke the tournament record for most points scored. The choir boys were tough. They had made their presence known in the valley.

Sit Down, Coach
By Ralphene

After some pretty heavy recruiting, David decided to sign with Stanford out of high school. His recruitment would make a story in itself—all the college coaches who sat in our living room to try to convince him to attend their schools. All the phone calls, fly-ins to meet at the airport just to try to change his mind, etc. He had taken his five trips to other schools and had narrowed the field to two schools, but Susie, who was a junior at Stanford, convinced him to at least come down and spend a weekend on the Farm. David worked out with Dave and Mark Schultz in the Stanford room for two days, and the rest is history.

No matter how good the wrestler, that next step is always a big one. Whether it be from junior high to high school, high school to college, college to open wrestling, it is like starting over again. So David's first collegiate dual match was a pretty big deal to all of us. Stanford was wrestling Oregon in Palo Alto. We all knew Coach Ron Finley from his involvement in AAU wrestling, and he always fielded a strong team in the Pac-10, so we were expecting a tight match.

Charlie and I had driven to Palo Alto with some friends to attend the match. We were sitting high up in the bleachers with Suz, watching the wrestlers warm up. Time for the match to start, and there is a delay. In a few minutes, Dave Schultz comes running up the bleachers to where we are sitting. He says, "Charlie, have you ever reffed a college match before?" Truth be told, Charlie had never reffed any match before. No occasion to—he was always coaching. However, his opinion was always highly valued by officials at every level.

Charlie says, "No, Dave, never have." Dave takes his whistle from around his neck and puts it on Charlie, and says, "You have now!"

The scheduled ref was a no-show for some reason, and somebody had to ref the match. Coach Chris Horpel and Coach Finley talked it over, and both agreed Charlie would be the logical person. Charlie had no problem with that, except that he would now have a bird's-eye view of David's first collegiate match. I must say, Charlie did an exemplary job, although no one was surprised by that. The evening went well, no problems, until the 165-pound match. David and his opponent took the mat. The match was fairly close, and at one point, and I do not remember the rule or technicality, Charlie called a one-point penalty on David. Chris Horpel got up from his chair and went to the scorer's table to talk to Charlie. He explained that this was a new rule change in effect this year. (And Chris was on the NCAA Rules Committee!) Charlie calmly said, "Sit down, Coach." Looked at the scorer's table and repeated, "One point penalty against the Stanford wrestler." Needless to say, the point stood. For some reason, nobody ever argued much with Charlie. He would have been in BIG trouble at home if David had lost that match by one point, I will tell you that!

That was the first and only match that Charlie ever reffed. He said he decided he couldn't go much higher than the Pac-10s, and he would quit while he was ahead!

Jake and Friends
By Ralphene

For several years Charlie and I drove back and forth from California to Maryland, where we had an apartment a couple blocks from Suz and Andy and the grandkids. We would spend six months in California, then six months in Maryland. We liked to be in Maryland during the school year to watch the grandkids' sporting events, school plays, concerts, etc. Soon we were spending at least seven months in Maryland. We really enjoyed our time in the D.C. area—for many reasons.

When we gave up our Maryland apartment for good and came back to California, Charlie was once again able to be involved with the BV wrestling program, although on a limited basis, of course. He would help in the room when he could, but when that became too difficult, Mike Lee would send a wrestler or two to our house to watch tapes, discuss strategy, and just talk wrestling in general with Charlie. Don't know who enjoyed it the most—the coach or the wrestlers!

Well, the first of the wrestlers to come was Jake Briggs. And that was the start of a wonderful partnership between Jake and Charlie. The first time Jake came over, he spent a few hours. He had planned to come back again a couple nights later at 6 pm.

That afternoon Jake called about five and asked if it was okay if he brought a friend along. Charlie said of course. Well, at six o'clock the doorbell rang, and when I opened the door, there was a line of people stretching way down the sidewalk! I can't recall everyone who was there, but I remember Kim and Jack, Mark Tucker, April and Randy, Grant, Landon, Shayne, and a couple others. They all said, "We hope you don't mind that we came along!" And we sure didn't mind. We had plenty of floor space. And David's room and our family room were kind of like a wrestling museum. Everyone wanted the tour! That was the first time we met that wonderful group of people, and we have been close friends ever since!

Jake Briggs learning from Coach Lee.

Never Be Late!
By Ralphene

In 1992, I was head pairings official for the Greco-Roman Olympic Trials, held in May of that year at the Concord International Greco-Roman Wrestling Tournament. The Olympics were to be held in Barcelona, and I had been assigned to work them.

As head official, it was my duty to conduct weigh-ins. As was the custom, weigh-ins were held Friday night from 5 to 6 pm at the team headquarters in the Concord Hilton Hotel. I sat at a registration table where the guys filled out their cards and then proceeded to another small room where the scales were. Simple enough—right?

Well, I was watching the clock on the wall in front of me, which had a minute hand that clicked as each minute passed, as well as a sweeping second hand. The hand clicked to six, straight up, and I started loading cards into my briefcase. I hear a commotion down the hall, and here comes a coach with a young man in tow. They run up to the desk, and the coach says, "My wrestler needs to weigh in." I was already looking at the clock, and my answer was, "Coach, technically weigh-ins are over. It is 22 seconds past six. I will weigh your wrestler in, but I can not guarantee that he will compete. That will be up to an Officials' Committee."

The Officials' Committee met, and after MUCH HEATED DEBATE—what do you think the decision was? The wrestler was not allowed to compete. He was late for weigh-ins. (I have a feeling that young man never missed a weigh-in again in his life!) Let me tell you, that decision has been kicked around a lot since then. However, I do believe it was the correct decision. Where exactly do you draw the line?

Now, it is a good thing this happened in 1992, and not eight years later, because the wrestler in question was heavyweight Rulon Gardner, a college kid at the time. Eight years later he pulled off the greatest upset in Olympic wrestling history when he defeated the great Alexander Karelin from Russia—a giant of a man who had NEVER lost a match. Rulon beat him 1-0 in the 2000 Greco-Roman Finals in Sydney. To make this story even more poignant, it was Karelin's final match. He had announced his retirement before the Olympics. In true wrestling fashion, he shook hands with Rulon, took off his wrestling shoes and left the shoes on the mat. (That is what wrestlers do when they know they have wrestled their final match.) There was not a dry eye in the house.

Let me tell you, from that day on, I used this story to impress upon my third graders what being on time or being late can mean!

I'll Bet Ya

As many would testify, my good friend Barry Rannells was not adverse to making a quite substantial monetary wager if he thought the odds were in his favor.

David was a high school junior in 1983. He was undefeated going into the Section Tournament. Yuba City had a kid named Rick Sakurada, also undefeated and quite a judo player. He pinned most of his opponents with throws and headlocks.

Barry was playing poker in Marysville and during the game, the subject of wrestling comes up. There were several sports buffs at the table and they all say what a tough wrestler this Sakurada kid is. Barry has never heard of this kid, of course. He starts talking about David. Well, I guess some of the guys at the table had heard of David, but probably had never seen him wrestle. Naturally, they have to make a bet. But it doesn't happen right then.

Barry comes over to our house with this story. He asks me what I think. I had never seen this kid wrestle, but I did know his record. But David was at an entirely different level. Barry asked if he could bet on David to pin the kid. I told him he would beat him for sure, but I couldn't guarantee a pin. I thought he probably would. That was good enough for Barry.

He goes back to Marysville and eventually finds the Yuba City guys. He proceeds to bet on the match. I think he had to bet that David would pin Sakurada in order to get the bet that he wanted. Well, it's one thing to beat a guy, but quite another to pin him. Sure enough, the two meet in the finals. Both are undefeated for the tournament and both have pinned all their opponents.

As you can imagine, there was a lot of hype on this match. To the average wrestling fan, Sakurada would look pretty darn good.

He pinned opponents with judo throws, which can be flashy. One thing David was not, was flashy.

David pinned the kid in the first period. (Lots of silent Yuba City Honkers now.) Barry was just giddy when he went to collect his money. That was the only time I know of that he made a bet on David—something you probably shouldn't do, but sitting around a poker table with a lot of loudmouths just aching to throw their money away on "their boy" was just too hard for a gambling man to resist!

P.S. I guess David never knew about the bet. I never mentioned it. There are a lot of different levels in wrestling. A good kid in junior high usually has an adjustment to make in a high school program. The kid who is a state champ in high school will have it tough in the Iowa wrestling room as a freshman. (I remember Cody saying he went 9-22 as a freshman at Nebraska.) The NCAA champ may find rough going in the Olympic Trials. There are a few kids who can step in as high school freshmen and dominate. Or can come into a big-time college program and do well.

David was one of those. He wrestled so many matches as a youngster, was exposed to so many situations, so many big matches, that psychologically any kid he wrestled was at a huge disadvantage. To Sakurada this was a big match. He was undefeated, but he had only wrestled local kids, maybe a kid or two from Clovis or San Jose. David had wrestled kids (literally) from all over the globe, in some high-pressure situations. And he had wrestled hundreds of matches. Sakurada knew nothing of this kind of competition. He had no idea what he was up against. He had no chance.

Records

Going through some old scrapbooks, I came across some notebooks that Ralphene had kept of David's wrestling career from his first match as a kid wrestler up until his last high school match. There are also most of his college and open matches, but not as complete a record as from age four years through high school. Each match, opponent, date, weight, location, age, and name of tournament or dual match was recorded.

As a kid wrestler David was 408-15. Two losses came as a result of injury forfeit. Eleven came while wrestling up at least one age group. One loss was to Terry Irwin from Susanville when both were nine. His other loss ended his 216-match winning streak. He lost a 5-5 criteria overtime match to Angel Varletta of Turlock in the finals of the Bay Area Championships.

In high school he was 176-9, with eight losses coming his freshman year. He also wrestled AAU and USWF, losing only twice. Once to John Heffernan in the quarter-finals of the Junior Nationals at UNI. (David came back to beat him soundly for third place.) He went on to defeat Heffernan in the Big Ten Championships in college. David also lost to Mike Van Arsdale, who went on to wrestle for Iowa State. David was the National Greco Champion that same year, but did not compete his senior year because of an injury.

Can you believe that Ralphene kept such complete records? It was great to go through them and remember many of those matches.

A Real Regret

When I first started coaching at BV, I had certain requirements the wrestlers had to meet in order to earn a varsity letter. You had to wrestle in at least eight matches and win half, or wrestle in at least eight matches and not get pinned.

At 138 pounds, for some reason, one year we had absolutely not a single body. So I put a certain kid at that weight. Now you had to see this kid to appreciate him. He was a scrawny redhead with freckles and wore glasses. He was smart as a whip and had the heart of a lion. But he could not wrestle a lick. He wrestled in every match that year, probably around 20 times. He did not win one match, but neither did he get pinned. That is, until the final match of the season. It was like it was scripted in a movie. The kid got pinned in the final period of his last match. I did not give him a letter. Something I will always regret.

Real Class

In the mid 1960s Earl Hicks and Lynn Mason were known as the "dynamic duo." A well-deserved name. They wrestled 145 and 154, or 154 and 165, and hardly ever lost.

At the Northern California Championships in 1967 both were undefeated. In the semis, Earl had to wrestle a blind kid. This meant he had to begin the match in a tie position—something Earl rarely did. Any time they broke free, they had to stop and tie up again. This style was very difficult for Earl, and consequently he lost a close match.

Many people, after the match was over, told Earl how unfair they thought it was, that he had to tie up. He never made that an excuse. In fact, he would tell those who said that, "How fair would it be to him not to tie up?" Now that is CLASS.

True Grit

Lynn Mason was BV's first State Champion. (At the time, it was just Northern California.) Lynn was the only wrestler I ever had who just never seemed to get tired. No matter how hard you pushed him, he just never ran out of gas. He was the same in football and was a terrific player. Driscoll and I used to talk about it. We never did figure it out.

At the Northern California Championships held in Sacramento in 1967, Lynn's senior year, Lynn had a great tournament. He went into the finals having beaten two really good wrestlers. In the finals, he was wrestling a kid from Poway who was undefeated for the year. The Poway kid was one point ahead in the second period when Lynn suffered a broken collarbone. He wrestled the final period with a broken collarbone and WON the match. They grew 'em tough in those days.

Poor Coaching

John Loomis was one of the very best wrestlers ever to wrestle in the Sacramento area. John deserved to win a state championship. I always felt it was my error that cost him one.

In John's senior year he was undefeated and in the section finals against Durbin Lloren of Tracy. Durbin was a fine wrestler who beat David for his only loss as a sophomore. But at this time John was the much better wrestler. It was the final period, and John was ahead by three points with three seconds to go, and he was on top.

The ref stopped the match and warned John for stalling. When they started in the down position again, Durbin somehow escaped and took John down to tie the match at the buzzer. John was so shaken that he lost in the overtime, so he took second.

My mistake was this—at that time, when you warned the top man for stalling, you did not stop the match. And, of course, with just three seconds to go, the match would have been over. Had I called a time out and pointed that out, John would have won. But who would think the kid could score an escape and takedown in three seconds?

John now came into the state tournament as the number-two cede, not the section champion. I was always matside whenever John wrestled. In the semi-finals, John's match was called at the same time as David's. Of course I went to the mat with David, and Bruce Summers went with John. David's match went the full six minutes, and he won. I hurried over to John's match. John was ahead by one point with ten seconds to go. He was wrestling a kid from Watsonville whom he had already beaten twice that year, by a comfortable margin each time. Just as time ran out, right AT the buzzer, the kid got a reversal. It was so close the ref could have called it either way, but he gave the other kid the two-point reversal. I have always felt that had I not made that oversight in the section finals, John would have been a state champion, because he would have come into the tournament on the other side of the bracket and I KNOW he would have beat that kid who beat him, in the finals. I don't think I ever explained this to John.

Bad Break

Sheldon Marr was one of the best wrestlers and nicest kids you would ever meet. He wrestled and beat Dave Schultz. Nuff said. He was also a several-time National Judo Champion. Unfortunately, Sheldon did not get to wrestle his senior year of high school.

It was November 1976, November 22, to be exact. We were scrimmaging another team in our wrestling room. Sheldon hit a kid with two or three nice throws, but on the last throw he sort of landed on his own head. He laid there awhile, but he could move around and talk, and after a minute or so he got up. I could tell he was still hurting, so I took him into the coaches' office, had him sit down, put an ice bag on him, and sort of massaged his neck and shoulder area. (Worst thing I could have done, it turns out.) The scrimmage was over, so I walked him out to his car and had a friend drive him home. As an afterthought, since I knew his dad was in the Air Force and he could go right to the base, I told him to stop and get it looked at since he still seemed to be in pain.

When they got to the base hospital, Shel went to get an x-ray, but had to sit around for about two hours and thirty minutes before he got it. Once the x-ray was read, the doctors came running, put him on a backboard, strapped him down, and took him to UC Davis Medical Center for surgery. Turns out he had badly fractured his sixth and seventh cervical vertebrae.

When the doctor asked him how this happened, Shel told him. He said the doctor did not believe him, especially when he said he had walked into the coaches' office on his own, and that I had rubbed his neck. The doctor told him he should be paralyzed or possibly dead, and that it was a miracle that he wasn't. The only thing the doctor could figure out was that his neck muscles were so strong from wrestling and judo, that must have been what saved him!

It took a long time, but Shel recovered and went on to compete again in judo. He won or placed in several national tournaments, and taught hand-to-hand combat to the Denver Sheriff's Department. He coached at Cherry Creek High School in the Denver area, and his teams placed in the top three in the state several times and were Colorado State Team Champions in 1991.

Right now he is considered to be one of the BEST martial arts instructors in the country.

Mike Salazar

Mike Salazar, that name evokes a lot of memories, most of them associated with wrestling, at which he excelled. I first became aware of Mike when he was a seventh grader at Carnegie Middle School. That probably would have been about 1971 or 1972. Carnegie had a fine wrestling program, and Mike was the best wrestler at the time. I don't remember just how it came about, but he began attending Bella Vista's wrestling practices. He did this during both his seventh and eighth grade years.

Upon entering Bella Vista as a freshman, he made the varsity team—no small achievement, considering the strength of the program. He went on to wrestle varsity for four years, as I recall, being the first wrestler to letter all four years.

In the finals of the league wrestling tournament his freshman year, held at San Juan High School, he was wrestling a senior from San Juan and was four points behind, with about thirty seconds to go. In practice we had worked on a wrestling move called the "three-second pin." It was a very flashy move, and none of our wrestlers had ever used it in competition. Mike was in the top position as they went out of bounds, stopping the clock with 25 seconds to go in the final period of the match. He looked at me as he came back to the center, and I yelled, "Mike, three-second pin!" As the wrestlers assumed the starting position, and the referee blew the whistle, Mike executed the move to perfection. It was wham, bam, PIN. Mike leapt to his feet, the BV crowd went wild, and Mike ran around the mat, jumping up and down in pure joy. The San Juan coach said he had never seen such an example of poor sportsmanship. BS—it was just a young man who had become a league champion as a freshman, showing his jubilation.

Mike did everything in a big way. He was an excellent practice-room wrestler who always tried to drill to the best of his ability and help his partner do the same. Drilling was something I spent many years trying to perfect with my teams. Mike was the first wrestler to grasp the concept of intense drilling.

I also had Mike as a physical education student. One day, I believe it was his junior year, we were conducting physical fitness tests. The whole class was standing around the pull-up bars, being tested on pull-ups, and Mike said, "Hey, Coach. Has anyone ever done a one-armed pull-up?" I said, "I think so," but what I was imagining was holding the bar with one hand and grabbing your wrist with the other and doing a pull-up. Many kids with good strength could do that. But what Mike was talking about was jumping up and grabbing the bar with one hand, hanging straight down with his feet off the ground, and pulling up with just one arm until his chin was over the bar. I said, "Let's see, Mike." And he did it! As far as I know, in my thirty-two years as a teacher at Bella Vista, he is the only one to be able to perform this feat of strength. When we would run into each other over the years, he always would say, "Hey, Coach, did anyone do a one-armed pull-up yet?" And the answer was always no. That move takes tremendous strength. To this day I do not know how he did it, but I saw it with my own eyes.

I got to know Mike and his family very well, having had Julian, his older brother, wrestle for me. Julian was a fine wrestler in his own right. Virginia was the Bella Vista hall monitor for a number of years and made the best tacos you have ever eaten! Mike's father, Julian, was a great supporter of his kids at Bella Vista.

By far the number-one factor that contributed to the success of the Bella Vista wrestling program was the establishment of the age-group club known as the Sacramento Super Stars. This group, it was safe to say, was the strongest age-group wrestling program in the country. I started out coaching the boys myself, but as the club began to increase in numbers, we decided we needed another coach. Mike was the one we chose, and it was a perfect fit. He had the enthusiasm and the conditioning to be able to wrestle with the boys, and the club really took off. We limited the group to twenty boys because of the size of the room, and we were selective because the talent level was so high. The high school team became very successful because of the outstanding kids' program the Super Stars provided. So in his own way, Mike could claim credit for much of the continued success of the high school program.

These four Super Stars were members of the 1979 World Schoolboy Wrestling Team. Back row: John Loomis, David Lee. Front row: Ken Gaudreau, Tracy Yeates.

Mike developed an interest in Greco-Roman wrestling, which fit his style and temperament because he was an explosive wrestler, with good upper-body strength and balance, and he showed absolutely no fear of upper-body throws. He was good enough to make the 1977 U.S. University World team and compete for the U.S. in the competition held in Las Vegas. I was fortunate to attend that tournament and watch Mike compete.

My association with Mike was always very positive. He was a neat guy. Age 52 is far too young to go. He will be remembered in the Lee household.

The Weigh-In

OK, Targe, here is the Casey Noland story. We were wrestling San Juan at their place. The rule was you had to weigh in between 5 and 5:30. So I have all my kids lined up ready to go. Now it was sort of an unspoken rule that when a wrestler from one team got on the scale, it was the coach from the other team who would say, ok, he made weight or not.

It was probably 5:05 when Casey stepped on the scale. The weight bar on the scale just sort of teetered between standing in the middle and touching the top. Well, the San Juan coach says Casey is over weight. He is really being picky, but that's ok. I told Casey to run a lap or two around the track right outside, spit a few times, and he would be fine.

Casey is the most conscientious kid around. He puts on three layers of sweats and hustles outside. When he came back in, he sat down on a bench right in front of the scale, which is right next to their towel room, and the coach was standing right beside the scale. I was looking at the clock which was one of those that clicked off the minutes. Casey finally got out of his sweats and started to step on the scale, which is maybe three feet away, just as the clock ticks to 5:30. The coach practically yanked the scale out from under Casey's feet and shoved it into the towel room and locked it. "Too late, he didn't make it." I cannot believe this. I can't remember much of what happened after that. Anyway, we forfeited the weight, lost the match by three points, and the two of us did not speak for three years. (That was another of our 28 losses.) I could not even stay in the same room with him. If he came into a ceding meeting, I left.

Here is the interesting story of how we again got on speaking terms. I don't think I have ever told this before.

San Juan was coming to wrestle at BV that year. I was coming out of the coaches' office and was just about ready to turn the corner when he came around the corner from the other direction. We practically ran into each other. Both of us were stunned, and we stood there just looking at each other for what seemed like two minutes, but was probably five seconds. I don't know why I did it, but I stuck out my hand and said, "Let's bury the hatchet." He took my hand; I don't remember if he hugged me, but he might have.

We were wrestling in the sub-sections that year, and going into the last day we were closer than Bush and Kerry, with Encina, going for the team title.

In the wrestlebacks for third place, a kid from San Juan was supposed to wrestle an Encina kid. The San Juan wrestler was upset over losing in the semi-finals, and he went home. The race for the team title was so close that every point counted, so if the Encina kid gets a forfeit, he picks up one point for that, plus place points.

Ralphene was keeping track of everything. She knew who wrestled whom, how many points they won by, who they would wrestle next, everything. She told me about the San Juan kid. I go to their coach and tell him. He apparently is not aware of this. I don't remember how he did it, but he got the kid back in time to wrestle the consolation match. The kid won, and Encina picked up no points there. I had a kid who placed fifth in the league tournament, so he qualified as an alternate. Most kids who are alternates don't bother to show up for the sub-section, and most coaches don't care. I always felt, "Leave no stone unturned." Sure enough, there is a kid in that weight who does not show up. So our alternate comes in and wins one match in the wrestlebacks to earn one team point.

So our making up, my insisting we take advantage of every opportunity, and marrying Ralphene paid off. WE BEAT ENCINA BY 1/2 POINT!

Pardner

Last night Ralphene and I attended the Sacramento City College Hall of Fame Sports Banquet. Mark Loomis and Bill Hickey were inducted. Mark was a State Champion for me in 1978, going 41-0.

I met Bill in 1962. He was the wrestling coach at El Dorado High School in Placerville. My first scrimmage as a wrestling coach was against Bill's team at Placerville, after which I was called on the carpet by my principal because I had broken some rule that said you could not travel more than 30 miles from home to scrimmage. I think it was 37 miles to Placerville, so I guess I did stretch the rules once in a while. We scheduled a home and home with El Dorado High School every year until Bill left to be wrestling coach at Sac City College.

One year BV put on a sixteen-team tournament. It was a pretty tough one. I had invited Bill's team, and he accepted. A few days before the tournament he found out he had to stay home and take charge of running a big jv tournament of his own, because his assistant was sick with the flu. It must have been going around, because four of his starters couldn't come to our tournament. He sent nine kids with his wife, Marylou. They won the tournament. Neither one ever lets me forget that.

Bill and I loved to fish. We needed an excuse to do more fishing, and to buy another boat, so we formed the Charliebill Guide Service. It was the first guide service on the American River. (I believe there are 52 now.) It lasted eight years. I could easily write a whole book just on some of those experiences.

It's said a person makes many friends in life, but is lucky if he has one real partner. Bill and I are still partners. We did a lot of things together for a lot of years. He just turned 70. It was good to see him and Lou last night.

Making the Grade

I had a certain kid come to me as a senior, and explain that as a freshman I had given him a C in PE. Was there any way he could bring that up to an A (three years later)? I said no way. I was thinking, I can't do this. But he was heartbroken, with just that one C on his perfect record. So I said OK, without checking with my principal or the registrar first. I told him he had to come every morning before school and run three laps around the green without walking, for ten days in a row. He could stop whenever he wanted, but he must not walk. If I ever caught him cheating, just walking so much as one step at any time, then all bets were off and he would keep the C. He agreed.

His mother brought him to school every morning. He completed eight days perfectly. This was really hard on him. He was short and very much overweight. He probably never ran a full green in his life before this. He would run about 20 or 30 yards, then stop to catch his breath. So it would take him a good hour to do it right. On the ninth day it rained—it really poured. The kid did not show up. He showed up the next day ready to run. I explained that the deal was off because he missed yesterday. He said, "It was raining." I say, "So what, you had to run ten days in a row." He begs and pleads. I give in again, only this time it is 20 days in a row. "Miss for any reason, get sick, break a leg, get shot, have a rock fall on your head—you are done. Understand?" He agrees. There were only 20 days of school left. Well, he made it. In fact, he got in such good shape after about ten days that I made little deals with him. If he could run the three greens in such and such a time, I would waive the rest of the greens. Well, he practically killed himself, but always just seemed to come up a little short. On the last day, his mother came with him and told me how wonderful I was and gave me a big box of homemade cookies. He ran his last three greens in his best time ever. When he started, he would have to stop at least 20 or 30 times.

So now I go to the registrar to change the grade, and she says she can't do it without the principal's okay. Now I'm thinking, great, what if Snelson won't change the grade? I've given the kid my word. He HAS to change it. So I go see Lloyd, and explain the whole deal. Thank goodness he said okay.

Ralphene and I were at Border's bookstore several years later when I ran into this young man. Even after all those years, I knew him. We say hi, and you know what the first thing he talked about was!

One That Got Away

Ben Campbell (now Senator Ben Nighthorse Campbell from Colorado) was a former national judo champion and coach of the Sacramento Judo Club. He was highly regarded and many athletes wanted to train with him.

A kid by the name of Doug Nelson, from Reno, came to the club, stayed there and trained. I had arranged for Ben to put on a judo exhibition at BV; I believe this was in 1966. When he came (and he always did a super job) he brought Nelson with him for demonstration purposes. I had the whole wrestling team there. I asked Ben if he would mind if one of my wrestlers rolled around the mat with Nelson. He said fine. I had Lynn Mason, a senior and one tough cookie, go a few rounds with him. No standing throws or anything like that, just mat work. Well, Nelson turns Mason every which way but loose. He pins him at will. I'm impressed. Now comes the good part. Campbell tells me the kid is only seventeen and will be a senior in high school next year. Ben asks if I would be interested in him coming to BV, since he had legal guardianship and BV was one of the schools where he worked. Here was a lock on a state champ! This kid had just wiped up the mat with one of the best wrestlers in the state. Well, as luck would have it, the principal wouldn't work with me to get him in. The kid ended up going to La Sierra. I don't think John Phillips, the La Sierra coach, ever knew anything about him. But at 17, and being the National Open Judo Champion, he was something else. If only you had been principal then, Targe!

5th Period Judocans

As a youngster, David met John Loomis, who got him interested in judo, and in turn, David got John into wrestling. John and David won several national titles each. As a result of David's involvement in judo, I took up the sport too. Ben Campbell was the instructor at the Sacramento Judo Club where I worked out. I stayed with it for about three years and earned a brown belt. Campbell was trying to get judo in the high schools but met with little success.

I thought it would be a good way to reach some of the kids who didn't like school and never dressed out for PE. You know the kids I mean. I approached Bob Atteberry, my vice-principal, with the idea, and he said it sounded pretty good. Only catch was, I wanted to have the same kids every day, fifth period, all semester, with judo being the only unit. He was a little hesitant about that but finally gave the green light. I had done a little homework and talked with many of the kids I wanted, so when we had signups I got the 20 kids I'd hoped for. Nineteen had never been exposed to judo. The one kid who was a real jerk, a big loudmouthed bully—I made sure he got in.

I bought gis for the kids and we started out. I insisted they embrace the spirit of judo, which means "gentle way." Bowing before entering the class, bowing to me, their "sensei" or teacher, not talking unless I said ok. It was a hard-sell at first, as this was not the best-behaved group of twenty kids.

About two weeks after we started the class, I had a group of judo players from Japan visit BV and observe our class. They were on tour, and I believe Kenny Santiago had arranged for a competition in Sacramento. They were 16 years and under National Judo Champions. Our kids were quite impressed. The kids asked some questions. The team had an interpreter, and it went well. The one question and answer that made a real impact was one the "class bully" asked their heavyweight. He asked why he did judo. This was just after their team leader explained that these kids all went to the same school and worked out twice a day, 364 days a year. (I still have a hard time believing that.) Well, the Japanese kid said, to everyone's surprise, that he really did not like judo all that much, but his father wanted him to do it.

That evening we watched this group of JUNIOR champions just tear up a group of black belts (older guys) from Northern California who Ken Santiago had assembled. After that it was like a movie script. Something in that experience got through to the "bully." He did a 180 and turned into one of the best kids in the class. The kids really got into it. Ben Campbell arranged some competitions with some area clubs and other schools. We kicked butt, as they say now. Campbell said he was going to enter us as a club in the Northern California Judo Championships to be held in June.

The kids were really looking forward to that since they had creamed all their competition. Sad to say, the script did not have a happy ending. Campbell was told he hadn't gotten the application in on time, so we were not allowed to compete. He said he thought it was because we had beaten everybody we sparred with. I was mad, and the kids were very disappointed. End of story. (That was the end of judo at BV. It was one of my best experiences ever. I'm sure those kids will never forget that year in fifth period PE.)

The Lavender Singlet
By Sheldon Marr

Ralphene recently asked me why I was wearing a lavender singlet in a picture from the 1976 California State Freestyle Championships...So, here's the story:

After the regular season ended my junior year, we started our freestyle season. Coach Lee ordered a bunch of singlets for us, and told us to come to his office and get one if we were going to compete in freestyle. I tried on a couple to see what size I needed, and told Coach I wanted either a black or a red singlet (our school's colors) in that size...

Instead, Coach threw me a purple singlet in my size, and said, "If you're gonna wrestle flashy, you might as well look flashy!!!" Actually, I didn't want the purple singlet, but Coach kind of insisted.

Well, it turned out to be pretty good luck, as I had an undefeated freestyle season, qualified for the California State Championships, attended the event with teammates Casey Noland, Russ Duke, and friend Joe Walker (Del Campo), and I won the tournament going 7-0 with 7 pins (the only one to do so in the tournament...) So again, I guess Coach was right!!!

Sheldon Marr in his lavender singlet in 1976.

Some Great Times

At breakfast the other day, Ken mentioned that his dad was quite sick, and it didn't appear that he would make it. Sad news indeed. I got to thinking of the first time I met Mr. Gaudreau, and all of the good times we shared throughout the years. We (Ralphene, Suz, David, and I) had been hitting the tournament trail for a couple of years. We got to know some neat folks. Mr. Gaudreau had been taking Eddie to some tournaments in the Bay Area, as had the Kitchens, Petersens, Wyatts, Wagners, and others.

The first time I saw Mr. Gaudreau (I don't know why, but I always referred to him as Mr. Gaudreau) he was sort of crouched over in a corner watching Eddie wrestle. Here was this short fella with a pretty-substantial belly hanging over his belt, going through all sorts of contortions. Of course, he was no different than most parents when their kid wrestled. We talked, and he knew David and me. He was soft-spoken and not one bit overbearing. He did not miss much when it came to his kids and wrestling. So all of us became friends. Since I was the "Coach" I arranged for these kids to have a practice time at BV. I would be in their corner at tournaments and just try to be helpful. I knew many of these boys might come to BV.

Eddie Gaudreau was a very good wrestler. One of the reasons he was as good as he was, was because his dad gave him every opportunity to be good. He brought him to Bella Vista to work out every chance he got. He bought him the best gear. He hardly ever criticized him if he lost a match. He was the "supportive parent" before the term became popular.

Once the Super Stars were formed, Mr. Gaudreau could not do enough for the club. Anything we needed, he would see to it we got. Best example: The club was going back to Lincoln, Nebraska for the AAU Nationals. It was a goal of the club to have every kid be a national champion. So as a parent you had to be prepared to do some traveling in the summer. (Most local kids and parents stopped wrestling at the conclusion of the regular season.) And you could not just go to the nationals, you had to qualify. This meant a lot of traveling. So Mr. Gaudreau bought a motor home for the team to travel in!! It was big enough to take the whole team to the various tournaments we went to around the country. (Some of those trips would make wonderful stories. Such as going through Wyoming in July and stopping at every fireworks stand with an excited group of young boys!)

Mr. Gaudreau always used to ask if I thought Kenneth would make the varsity as a freshman. Ken only weighed around 75 pounds, wringing wet. Eddie had enjoyed such success that he wanted Ken to have the same experiences. He was just sure that Ken would never make 95 pounds. I told him not to worry, that Kenny would beat most 95-pounders if he only weighed 60 pounds. I said Kenny reminded me of a ferret when he wrestled. Quick and deadly.

Mr. Gaudreau loved a good steak and a bottle of Lancers Chianti. Many's the time we finished off more than one bottle of the "good stuff" after everyone had left the motor home to go watch wrestling. I can still hear him in that high-pitched voice, and his rapid way of talking. "Go, Kenneth, take him down! Look out, take him down, come on now, hustle, be careful, that's it! Whew, Coach Lee, that one was close, but he didn't do too bad, do you think?"

He was one of the most likable people I have ever met. He was always upbeat. Never said a bad word about anybody. Lived for his family. I truly did enjoy being around Mr. Gaudreau.

Your Questions
More questions posed by Targe

Tough to say who was the best wrestler after David. David, of course, was not the best in every category. Trying to pick a best in the following categories was real tough, and I had to list several kids as equal.

Best overall wrestler: David Lee. He was just so sound and mentally tough, wrestled so many matches, beat so many tough kids—he is #1. #2 This is really a hard one. I could not pick between Lynn Mason, John Loomis, Mark Loomis, Vic Henderson, Cody Olson, or Tracy Yeates.

Best practice-room wrestler: Wes Gaston, Ken Gaudreau, Cody Olson, John Henderson

Worst practice-room wrestler: Mark Loomis, period. No one else even close.

Indefatigable: Mike Lee. He was just so consistent each match. When he went off the mat he ALWAYS RAN back to the middle, never took a breather, put the pressure on the other guy all the time. I can remember many matches when his opponent literally had to crawl back to starting position. Mike stands out because he beat so many kids who were better than he was, but he just pushed them until they broke.

Best team leader: Ken Gaudreau. He was always upbeat and seemed to know what I wanted from the team each match. His positive attitude and exuberance made the difference in more than one dual and tournament. Right with Ken would be Casey Noland.

Best pinner: David Lee, Mark Loomis.

Best takedown wrestler: John Loomis, Earl Hicks, Tony Kitchen, Ron Alera, Ken Gaudreau, Tracy Yeates, and Wes Gaston. These kids were real slick and fun to watch.

Best from the bottom: Mike Lee (because of the effort and hustle), Mike Salazar (explosiveness), David Lee (too much knowledge and experience to cope with, no one could hold him down).

Best rider: Larry Vasquez. When he beat Petrachek from San Juan 1 to 0 in the dual meet, it was the best example of riding ever for a BV wrestler.

Most memorable matches and wrestlers:

David Lee: The finals of the 1982 State Tournament, being on his back for 45 seconds and coming back from behind to win his first state title as a sophomore.

David Lee: His win over Junior Taylor at the Coast Classic as a sophomore. Taylor was a three-time Oregon state champ and a World and USWF National Champion.

Barry Alan: Not the most talented wrestler— who came to see me and wanted to quit because of the pounding he took everyday from Vasquez in the wrestling room. But he hung in, and I can see like it was yesterday when he beat the San Juan kid who was so much better than he was. Barry will never forget that match.

Mike Whiting: Not getting pinned against Placer, enabling us to win the match. My most enjoyable dual win of my 22 years of coaching.

Vic Henderson: Losing in the finals of the 1974 State Championships to Fred Bohna of Clovis High School, coached by Dennis DeLiddo. Vic was ahead by 4 points with 39 seconds to go in the match, with both men on their feet. I hollered at him to keep attacking, so he shot, and Bohna caught him with a front quarter nelson. They stayed in that position until time ran out, at which point the ref awarded a two-point takedown and a three-point near fall, giving Bohna a 5-4 win. I was dumbfounded, because the ref never indicated the two points until the match was over. I thought they were neutral. I thought the Henderson clan was going to kill the ref! Fred Bohna went on to win an NCAA wrestling title at heavyweight for UCLA in 1979.

Casey Noland: In the 1977 state finals at American River College. He had wrestled an outstanding tournament, and had beaten some kids he shouldn't have. He was wrestling Jackson Kistler, Southern Section Champion and one of the best wrestlers in the country. Casey was ahead by one point and on the bottom. He was in a position to win the match—I can still see this as plain as day—when he reached back with his left arm to whizzer, and Kistler slapped a half nelson on him and put him on his back for three points and the match.

Mike Salazar: His match in the finals of the league tournament as a freshman. He was wrestling a kid by the name of Randy Vigil, a senior. Mike was behind in the third period. We had worked on a move called the "three-second pin." I hollered to Mike to try it. He hit it perfectly and pinned Vigil. Mike jumped up and ran around the mat in pure celebration. The San Juan coach never liked Mike after that.

Paul Ashnault: In the finals of the league tournament Paul beat Glenn Cooper of San Juan, the defending state champion and winner of 72 straight matches. Ashnault won 10-7.

Mike Lee: Beating the huge wrestler from Grant who threw Mike around like a rag doll for two periods, but Mike pushed him so hard that halfway through the third period the kid could hardly crawl back to the center of the mat and Mike turned him over like a pancake and pinned him.

Jerry Petersen: A member of the Super Stars who was just an average athlete but worked hard and took coaching very well. He was a smart wrestler and was much better than he looked. Many opponents would look at his physique and underestimate him. He surprised a lot of kids. Jerry graduated from Columbia, and the last I heard, was coaching wrestling at a high school in New York.

The Salazar brothers: Julian was the oldest and enjoyed a fair amount of success, a much better-than-average wrestler. Mike started to work out with us when he was a seventh grader at Carnegie. He was BV's most flamboyant wrestler, hands down. You loved him or hated him. He was a great practice-room wrestler and was a section champion.

The Kitchens: Scott wrestled for BV for two years after transferring from Folsom. He was a good wrestler who won the sub-section and placed fifth at state—one of the best kids in Sacramento at his weight. Tony was another of the Super Star kids. He was extremely talented, but had quite a temper. After a loss at an early age, he tried to flush his wrestling shoes down the toilet, and declared he would never wrestle again. He was a challenge to coach. When we would go on a trip, he had to ride with me. I made him listen to my music, which he hated, but I told him it would make him tougher because he could take it out on his opponents. He almost always won, so it became easier to get him in my truck without too much complaining. Tony deserved to win his state championship in 1986. He wrestled from age five with the Super Stars.

Next I pick my All-Time BV team.

My All-Time Dual Meet Team

It was very tough to pick just one kid at each weight for this. Ralphene suggested I pick three at each weight, and that would be hard. But I am going with just one. The weight classes are different today. The weights I am using are the ones that were in effect when I started coaching. I am picking what I think would be my best dual meet lineup. This does not necessarily mean the kid was the BEST at that weight. For example, John Loomis was probably the best 95-pound wrestler, but I am putting him elsewhere for overall team strength. I'll bet that if you picked 100 different people who are familiar with BV wrestling, not one would pick this lineup.

Charlie's All-Time Dual Meet Team

95#	Tracy Yeates
103#	Ken Gaudreau
112#	John Loomis
120#	Casey Noland
127#	Richard Hansen
133#	Lupe Rangel
138#	Jack James
145#	Earl Hicks
154#	Lynn Mason
165#	David Lee
175#	Mark Loomis
191#	Cody Olson
Hwt	Vic Henderson

Wouldn't it be fun to have a lineup like that all at one time?

Matchup

I can remember every kid on my first wrestling team (1963) and every one on my last (1984). Let's see how they would do in a match.

Weight	1963	1984	Result
95	Jim Whaley	Tony Kitchen	toss-up
103	Harvey Olson	Dan Tennant	toss-up
112	Ron Alara	Ken Gaudreau	Gaudreau by decision
119	Richard Hansen	Jon Lassiter	Hansen by fall
127	Gordon Leighton	Sam Tichenor	Leighton by decision
133	Jon Esparza	Todd Gaston	Gaston by decision
138	Ron McCaully	Mike Mahon	McCaully by decision
145	Ron Scott	Chris Richards	Scott by decision
154	Gene Ernst	Willy Kalb	Ernst by fall
165	Tony Rangel	David Lee	Lee by fall
175	Joe Prandini	Cody Olson	Olson by fall
191	Carl Kuhl	Jerry Petersen	toss-up
Hwt	Dave Jones	Mike Whiting	Jones by fall

Final result: The 1963 team would win this dual match by a score of 30-15, with three matches being toss-ups.

Wrestling

1963 Bronco wrestling team; BV's first Varsity Champions in any sport.

1984 Broncos; Sac-Joaquin Section Champions.

My first team went 8-2, losing twice to Roseville. They were BV's first varsity championship team in any sport. My last team went 20-0 and won the section.

Beyond High School

I am trying to remember the kids who wrestled for me and then went on to wrestle in college. It's 2:45 am, so I'd better not ask Ralphene for her help. When she wakes up, I'll add any she remembers who I might have forgotten. Junior college does not count.

Gordon Leighton-San Jose State
Mike Gallion-West Point
Lynn Mason-Wyoming
Barry Boustead-Naval Academy
Ed Gaudreau-Columbia
Ken Gaudreau-Columbia
Jerry Petersen-Columbia
Cody Olson-Nebraska
Tracy Yeates-Boise State
Wes Gaston-Idaho State
Mark Loomis-LSU/Bakersfield
John Loomis-Bakersfield/Oklahoma State
Casey Noland-Oregon State
Vic Henderson-UCLA
David Lee-Stanford/Wisconsin

All of these programs are strong. No average wrestler would get in. In most cases, wrestling is what got these kids admitted. Most took advantage of that, and came away with a college degree.

1979 Bronco wrestling team. C.A.L. Champs, N.E. Sub-Section Champs, Sac-Joaquin Section Champs.

Wrestling

Coach Lee's Legacy to His Wrestlers

By Eddie Gaudreau
written for Coach Lee's Memorial Service
December 26, 2010

"Leadership is a matter of having people look at you and gain confidence, seeing how you react. If you're in control, they're in control."

—Tom Landry

Thoughtful Observation—We all remember Coach on the sidelines with his notebook, writing, more than yelling instructions, in the heat of the match. When instructions were given, his was usually the only voice I heard when I was on the mat.

Individual Feedback—That same notebook was visible at the next practice when he recapped every match for each wrestler, win or lose. There was always some observation that could, if heeded, improve one's performance the next time out.

Motivator—How many of us wanted to win more for him than we wanted to win for ourselves?

Disciplined Practice—Coach was a student of the sport, and he brought his knowledge to the room every day through regimented practices that kept us at the top of our form.

These are a few of the traits I believe are required to coach successfully in any sport. Most impressively, he coached his own son to success at the highest levels of the sport. Anyone who has tried to coach their own children and have them listen, knows how difficult that can be.

In the first match of the league championships my senior year I found myself in a most interesting situation. A second string Del Campo wrestler had managed a tie at the end of regulation. This wasn't supposed to happen since my real goal was the state championship. At this point, everything for which we had worked so hard was in jeopardy. If I ever needed to hear from Coach Lee, this was it. When I got to the corner Coach had a very simple message, "Well, you got yourself into this. I think you know how to get yourself out." That certainly wasn't what I expected to hear, but I realized at that moment he was right. The rest of the longest minute in my wrestling career was spent in silence, and I never wanted to win more than at that moment. And that's the point—at that moment he knew what would motivate me. He had coached me for years, but at that moment he shifted the responsibility to me, and I cannot thank him enough, and I will never forget.

We all were able to look at Coach and gain confidence. When we saw that he was in control, we were able to take control. He was able to draw out the best in us.

Letter from Cody Olson
To support Charlie's nomination for a Lifetime Achievement Award at the University of Iowa, February 1, 2011

Mr. Steenlage, I am writing this letter to endorse Dr. Tom Buroker's nomination of Charles Lee for the Iowa Athletic Department Lifetime Achievement Award.

I was fortunate to be a small part of Coach Lee's life and a member of his last high school wrestling team. During the last month of the 1983 school year, my father gave me the opportunity to improve myself by allowing me to transfer to Bella Vista High School and to participate in the great tradition of Bella Vista wrestling! I had previously wrestled in Nevada and had some success, but to move into the tradition that Coach Lee had created opened many doors that would not have been opened had I stayed in Nevada.

My time at Bella Vista, with Coach Lee, was the best time of my life! Even though I didn't win that year's state tournament, I learned much about myself and became a better person. Each of the athletes who worked with Coach Lee has their own stories of how he touched their lives and made them better people. Coach didn't cut corners. He was truthful, and if you didn't want to hear the truth, you shouldn't ask him the question. I think Coach Lee was more in the business of creating character and molding young men into responsible people than creating state and nationally-ranked competitors. The byproduct was that we worked hard and wanted to do our best for ourselves, our families, and Coach Lee. We wanted to make him proud!

He was a man of few words, but what he said motivated the heck out of his athletes! An example of this sticks out in my mind—it was the consolation semi-finals of the state tournament. I had just earned the points to go into overtime, and there was a one-minute break. Coach Lee stated, "You will earn more scholarship money with a third place than with a fifth place finish." As simple as that may sound, it motivated me, and I still remember that thought. With that third place and having Coach Lee talking with college coaches on my behalf, I was offered and accepted a scholarship to the University of Nebraska.

Coach Lee hasn't been my coach for twenty-six years. I was lucky to have been part of his team and of the "Bella Vista Tradition" for one year. That tradition is still legendary in the Sacramento area to this day, and when I mention wrestling and Bella Vista, I am always asked if I wrestled for Coach Lee. I then do my best to make certain to explain how big of an influence he has been in my life and career! Thankfully, my parents thought enough of me to give me the chance of a lifetime and experience the "Bella Vista Tradition" and the tutelage of Coach Lee. It has given me an identity that I am very proud of: I wrestled for Coach Lee, and I was a Bella Vista Bronco!!

Sincerely,

Cody Olson

Cody's record during his one year at Bella Vista was 51-1. He placed third at the state meet at 175 pounds. He currently referees on a national level.

Letter from Barry Boustead
October 22, 2006

Just a footnote to the comments regarding Charlie's wrestling teams. I wrestled for him during the late 60s (I graduated in 1970). And while I was not one of the best he ever coached, his motivation did get me an appointment to the Naval Academy where I graduated in 1974. His leadership and commitment also contributed to a love for the sport that continues to this day.

I have been involved in coaching (I am an airline pilot so it was always kids' clubs) and running tournaments for over 20 years here in Texas. This year we will celebrate the 10th anniversary of the Lone Star Duals (a national high school and college tournament) which both Iowa and Iowa State have attended, and I am the Tournament Director for the 41st National Wrestling Coaches Association All-Star Classic on November 20th at the Dallas Convention Center Arena. The Lone Star Duals has provided scholarships for many kids to continue on to college, and was the site of Cael Sanderson's win that pushed him beyond Dan Gable's NCAA record in 1999.

All of this is a result of my exposure to Charlie at an important time in my life. My experiences wrestling for him during those years have provided motivation for much of what I have accomplished in my life and taught me many important lessons about tenacity and overcoming adversity that I have used many times over the last 36 years. I am hoping to pass that knowledge on to kids through my involvement in the sport today. I would bet that most, if not all, of his wrestlers feel the same way.

By the way, I can remember many of the matches we had against Bill Flake's teams, and I don't remember that we lost any—I can imagine his frustration!

Sincerely,
Barry Boustead

Barry dedicated the 2011 Lone Star Duals Tournament to Charlie and his Navy coach, Ed Perry. This is a quote from the program:

2010 saw the loss of several important wrestling figures, both in my life and in the sport. My two coaches both passed away this year and the loss will be great to the wrestling community. Coach Charlie Lee, father of NCAA Champion David Lee, was the longtime coach of Bella Vista High School in Fair Oaks, California. Hired as a football coach after being a member of the 1959 Iowa Rose Bowl team, Charlie became a tremendous asset to the sport of wrestling in the state of California. He was inducted into the California Wrestling Hall of Fame, along with his wife Ralphene, and his son, David. Interestingly, there are two additional prior wrestlers of Charlie's here this year, NCAA Officials Cody Olson and Kenny Gaudreau. Cody has been here for most of the competitions, and this is Kenny's first year to participate.

Coach Ed Perry, long-time Navy coach, was a three-time NCAA Champion and won the last 3 of 9 titles his family took (out of 9 possible). Both Ed's father and brother won the 3 titles they were eligible for and contributed to unquestionably the greatest run of any single family in NCAA history. Ed was the head coach at Navy when I arrived as a Plebe in June of 1970. Although an injury forced me out of competitive wrestling at Navy, Ed nevertheless had a great impact on my life. Without the presence of Charlie and Ed in my formative years, I don't believe this event would have come about, and I am dedicating this year's event to the two of them.

1970 CVC Champs

Coach Lee
Letter by Casey Noland, April 16, 2014

Coach had such an incredible impact on my life! I can hardly believe it as I look back. He has always been a role model during my career as a wrestler, a coach for twenty-five years, and a teacher for twenty. I also had the unenviable challenge of following him as the coach of the BV wrestling team for two years.

I first met Coach when he came sauntering in to the Andrew Carnegie Gym sometime in 1971. He was the coach at Bella Vista HS, and I was wrestling for his beloved feeder program, the Andrew Carnegie Scots. My coach was Sebastian Adorno, a great coach in his own right. Charlie was a very large and gentle giant. Later I would find out that he was a Rose Bowl lineman for the Iowa Hawkeyes and played with the likes of Alex Karras.

Of course, as a young 7th grader I had no idea who this man was. To me he was Coach Lee, my brother Chad's high school wrestling coach. Chad would come home with all these tales about the "larger-than-life coach"…Coach Lee. The amazing thing was that there were all these legends from guys who wrestled for him.

This was the genius of Coach Lee. He brought each of us wrestlers into his lineup like a crazy cast of characters. He mysteriously knew how to do that. Each wrestler's seat, bag, and uniform were special and unique. There was no disrespectful interchange. Each team member had to be in his special place of honor. Coach Lee understood the pageantry and prestige. He was crafty about this. Early on, he had his guys in robes. He brought HONOR to each and every seat on that bench. Missing one piece of your uniform was unthinkable and to be over weight, a travesty. There was no trying and trying again. You lined up, filed up, no talking, and you made weight the first attempt.

Each infraction was met with a satirical and immediate correction. "Oh, your hair's too long, let me trim it for you." A sense of humor, few words, and an immediate correction of the problem. The pride and detail in each letterman's jacket back then is beyond belief now.

One story: We're in the BV locker room immediately after weigh-ins, and our 165-pounder is a big, obnoxious kid. Coach Lee walks directly over to him, grabs his brown paper bag, kind of rips it out of the wrestler's hands and bangs it down, boom into the bottom of the empty metal trash can. Swift, sudden, abrupt, and then Coach is GONE! We all stood there in shock. What was that? No speech, no calling him aside, no great explanation, just bam!

Coach Lee could have been a psychologist. Now, how come I remember that as if it were yesterday? Who knows what that teammate did? Was he over-stuffing himself? Was he not thinking

Wrestling

about the big match we had in about one hour? Not sure, but I will never forget it. I think the message to me was, "Stop fooling around, stuffing your face with food you do not need, we have a HUGE match coming up in one hour." I never heard an explanation. We wrestlers never discussed it, that was just it—bam!

Another story: My senior year after wrestling season, I'd been recruited by several major colleges and had scholarship offers from several. Many days throughout high school I would show up at school around 7 am, and there was Coach, typing our stats and posting them for all to see on the coaches' office window. This time Coach greets me with his usual, "Hello, Miles," and invites me to have a seat. Then he asks me how things went yesterday. Well, the day before, my best friend and fellow teammate and I had decided to be "Big Men," and we showed up at the Honors Society Picnic at the park like two fools, with two beers in a sack. I had NEVER done anything this stupid in my life, but I did that day. Coach Lee just says, "Heard you were at the park yesterday." That's it. He never lectured me about the foolishness of drinking, the incredible stupidity of my actions, the laws or ordinances I had broken. I felt an inch tall! I wanted to crawl out of the building and slither on down the street, I felt so low. Coach never said another word. End of story.

That was Coach Lee, man of few words…but a man of a few small "choice" words. And man could he motivate me! Like none before and none other to this day. He knew just what to say to motivate me onward and upward. I would get so mad at his words that I would work just that much harder.

I lost to Joe Walker of Del Campo High School 9 of 10 times we wrestled. I'd come off the mat and be thinking, "Okay, Coach, just say something profound, so I know how to beat this guy in the future." No, Coach would just say something like, "He's just better than you." Oh, that would make me so mad! I'd go back in the wrestling room and work ten times as hard, because I wanted to beat Joe Walker 100 times worse now. I kept shooting in on a bad double, and Joe would pancake me every time (I finally figured that out). Joe had a mean headlock. Would Coach Lee get down on the mat and work on a "pancake" with me? No, he'd just tell me Joe was better than me. That's it. Coach knew how to motivate us.

I loved wrestling for him, to the point that I wanted to win just to make him happy. That's love, honor, and respect! That's motivation. I wrestled in college for one of the winningest coaches in NCAA history, and he was a tremendous man and coach in his own right. But Coach Lee was the greatest coach I ever knew, or wrestled for, or was even remotely acquainted with. Most of my coaches were good men, and they showed me stuff. I liked the team but no one, except Coach Lee and Sebastian Adorno, my junior high school coach, made me want to win so much and want to work so hard.

The truth is I loved Coach Lee. He never yelled, never put us down, never said a bad word about anyone. He just made us want to do well and taught us integrity, respect, honor, and dedication. Another thing he used to do for me on those early morning office visits or chats (and yes, they were short, but still medicine for my soul), was to give me a book or video or article by one of "The Greats." He was always putting great people before us. He posted sayings by Vince Lombardi around the room, or he would give me a book about Dan Gable. I'd go home, eat those books up, bring them back, and he'd give me something else. Coach Lee was a motivator! He was always investing in us. Investing in the total person.

Our wrestling room had three very important things in it: pictures, the chin-up bar, and a rope. The rope and the chin-up bar were the true avenues to the physical prowess we would need. The pictures…oh, the pictures. He had huge pictures of his top former wrestlers up on the wall, guys who'd won the Sections (CIF Masters) or guys who had placed in the Nor Cals (back then we didn't have a state tournament). I would look up at those pictures everyday, idolize those guys, and want in the worst way for my picture to be up there. Coach Lee gave us a goal and gave us motivation to be good. You see, our uniforms meant something! Everyone wanted to wear that Red and Black, (and White). It was something you had to earn though. It wasn't just handed to you. And, he didn't put some tiny little picture up. Coach Lee put up 24 x 30 inch pictures! They were HUGE, and everyone could see them. I wanted to be up on that wall!! BADLY…!

Just his physical presence was awe-inspiring. He stood over 6'4" tall and weighed 250 pounds or more. He was fast and agile for a big man, and he dressed down every day for wrestling practice, and he would wrestle with us. It was more like a bear playing with cubs. He would get down on his knees and show us stuff on the mat, never on the feet much, because we had a tiny wrestling room, guys falling all over each other. It's a wonder more guys didn't get hurt. He would get down on the mat and show us moves. He always had a new "trick move" each year. One year he taught us all the "three-second pin." Only Mike Salazar could learn it and use it. We always started practice with a warm-up, circling up, and then he would call us in, show us something. Then we went to work with our partner on it. Simple, straight forward, and to the point. We were to drill "on your own." He would move around and keep us going.

Matches and weigh-ins: At matches, there was a very strict protocol. First, at weigh-ins, everyone had to be in line in exact order by weight. If you were over, you were "off the team." Plain and simple. He was NOT going to fool around with people being over weight. He was notorious for this. Today, teams mingle around, out of order, half the squad over weight, coaches making excuses for kids, NOT COACH LEE! He was the consummate professional. You had better be on weight, and you had better be on time, and you had better be in line. That was your spot. It was an honor to have it. See today, lots of coaches put all their wrestlers together, big room and tons of assistant coaches. Not at BV! At BV, he was the only coach in the room, no assistant, no grad student, nothing. Coach Summers would be with us in the preseason while

Coach Lee was still out at football, but as soon as football ended, the junior varsity went up to the jv–freshman room. You had to EARN being in the varsity room and only about 15 guys were picked. We had 13 weights, and then he would usually pick a couple of extra big guys to be in the room for extra workout partners. What were we learning? It was an honor to be in the spot! You challenged early in the season, you earned that spot, and then you worked your butt off to keep it.

He also had this nice cute little trot he would do. He'd trot around the wrestling room making short little wise comments like, "Okay boys, let's keep moving." Or something like that. However, the point was: no big talks, no big lectures, no huge analysis, just keep moving. I think it was his plan to get us in shape by keeping us moving the entire practice. To this day, I'll go out to football practices and inevitably there are 50, 60, or 70 guys standing around. Not Coach Lee. We were in there, out of there, short and sweet, and we never stopped moving once the practice really got underway. (Note: That could have been due in large part to the fact that he wanted to get home to the "Redhead." He was a devoted family man, and in large part he was compartmentalizing wrestling. We will work hard. We will have a great team, but I am getting done with this and going on home to David, Susie, and Ralphene.) I don't remember a single three-hour practice ever. We were usually out of there by 4:30 pm. Of course, he got it set up so that we had 6th period PE. We all took PE together, and so we got started around 2:30 pm. In the winter we would start getting out of there by 4 pm. Short and sweet.

So, what was he modeling? Family is important. We will be good at wrestling, but wrestling is NOT everything! Coach used to tell me, "I'll go watch anything that is excellent." Some guys were big and tough and too cool for the opera or the ballet. Not Coach. If it was "excellent," he didn't care what it was, he wanted to see it. He would pick out some of the nerdiest, brainiest kids in school and would be in the office playing chess with them daily. Coach had a lot of interests. What was he modeling? It's important not to be just a dumb jock. It's important to get an education, to be a gentleman, and to know something about life, not just wrestling! Also to be interested in other people and what they were doing. If the best ice skaters in the world were going to be in town that night, he was interested and would try to make it. When David and Susie went on to school, it was Stanford, because not only did Stanford have good wrestling, but it also had the best academics!

Coach Lee was truly interested in people and life. Each summer he went to Montana or Idaho to fish. He loved fishing, and he later became a guide. He shared that with the guys at BV, and many of the staff would go on big fishing trips with him each summer. Sometimes he would just go by himself. Later in life he told me all about the Madison River in Montana. He told me step-by-step, turn-by-turn, how to get to the best places on the Madison, and I went. My son and I will never forget the day we stood fishing all day, by ourselves, on the Madison River. He told us the exact fly to use there (after he had taught my boys and I how to fly fish).

There were better teams for sure. Merced and Steve Sanchez's group at the time was technically superior to us. They were definitely a better tournament team. But we were probably a better dual team…top to bottom, we rarely had a hole. A forfeit was unthinkable. It just didn't happen! Del Campo and San Juan programs were close to being as good as ours. Don Crowl at San Juan and Joe Cavallaro at Del Campo were our fierce rivals. We did not hate them, but we greatly disliked each other when it came to Match Night. They had full line-ups: varsity, jv, and freshman…39 kids just like BV. We had some incredible matches. One night I think we had close to 2,000 people at Del Campo. The spotlight was on, and we had a barn-burner. Match-by-match, down to the wire every time, with the outcome depending on the "poor heavyweights." It was exciting and fun. The parents, student body, and fans loved it. Most of the families were in the stands, and every family was represented. We had a great group of guys and families, and Coach Lee was our leader, no question. Parents rarely questioned, nagged at, or second-guessed him. Maybe my dad (the attorney) did, after Joe Walker defeated me nine out of ten times, but that was about it. Coach Lee simply said, "Your dad is so frustrated because Joe Walker has beaten you so many times." Coach Lee would grin and laugh and that was it.

One time when I was in for a morning chat and complained about my dad being overbearing at times, Coach Lee's response was amazing. "I think you are fortunate to have the dad you have." And that was it. SLAM the Door! Case closed! End of story! That was what he modeled. Don't whine and complain about your family! Be thankful and make the best out of it. That was it. He had reason to chime in and join my chorus, but he DIDN'T. Never ever, not one time. Coach Lee controlled his tongue. I don't know if that was intentional. Don't know if he worked at it. All I know is that he was totally a man of integrity and NEVER said one negative word about me, my dad, or my family. If I had been the coach, I would have been tempted to say some things, but HE DID NOT! He modeled integrity!! Sometimes his silence was deafening, and I hated it. It frustrated me, but it forced me to figure things out and stop whining and complaining! He wasn't perfect, but whatever happened, he modeled integrity and controlling the tongue. This applied to other teams and coaches as well. I never heard a negative word come out of his mouth, even about his fiercest rivals.

In a way, to talk about Coach's accomplishments is to miss the point. Coach Lee was far more to us than a successful coach and athlete, as far as wins and losses go. Coach Lee truly was a respected man, a tremendous role model, mentor, and ultimately a friend.

As Tim Driscoll, son of Don Driscoll, our football coach at Bella Vista for many years, said at Coach's memorial service, "Most of all, Charlie was a friend." Think of that—Tim grew up as a little kid knowing Coach Lee as the "Gentle Giant." Yet, Tim's most vivid memory of Coach was as a friend. Coach treated us with respect and let us go on to be men. He knew when to draw the line, stop coaching, and move on to an adult relationship.

During the last few years of his life I got to be around him a lot. Things were not working out for me at that time, and my dad was gone, so I went to Coach from time to time to seek his advice, hang out, and take him fishing. He'd call me up and ask me about the job hunt. We'd go fishing and then go get something to eat. He always insisted on paying. We shared some great times together, and we had some incredible talks on those fishing outings. On some of those outings, my son Cody would come along, and Coach taught him to fly fish. He also insisted on purchasing some of the gear, starter gear to get us going. During these trips I would tell him about my struggles and having to start all over, etc. Guess what Coach would say… "It's just money." It was kind of like, "Joe Walker is just better than you."

He was saying to me, in large part, "Just go for it! All you can do is lose. It's not the end of the world. Just get back up, start over. That's life! No big deal." He was so funny when telling me, "I wanted to buy a town in Montana. Ralphene wouldn't let me…. darn. I really wanted to buy that town."

His GMC truck. I'll never forget that truck. In 7th grade, I started calling Coach Lee on Friday nights in the springtime and asking, "Coach, can I ride with you to the tournament tomorrow?" Always kind and gracious, "Sure, be here at 6 am." My parents would drive me to his house, and off we would go, usually to BAWA. (Bay Area Wrestling Association.) Sacramento didn't have tournaments then, so we had to travel to BAWA to get matches in the spring, during freestyle. Ralphene and Charlie would sit up front, and David, Susie, and one or two of my friends and I would ride in the back of the pickup. It was fun, and we didn't have a bunch of adults doting over our every move. Wow, things were different then!

One of the amazing things about BV in the 1960s, 70s, and 80s, was the camaraderie amongst the coaching staff. Coach Lee loved the men he worked with, and they coached football, basketball, wrestling, and track together. If they didn't coach, they assisted in other ways. They ran the scoreboard for each other. I remember Coach Lee being at basketball games religiously to assist Pisto (Gordon Pistochini), our basketball coach. Anyway, they ALL coached football together. One of the interesting cast of characters was Larry Fletcher. One night at a basketball game, Larry and Coach decided to have some fun. A young reporter from a radio station had left his recorder sitting at the scoring table while going to get a Coke at half time. Larry decided to interview Coach.

It was in the early 1960s that the legend began. "Coach Lee," as we always called him, gradually built his program as Bella Vista, a new school, progressed. The team was solid all through the 1960s, fielding full varsity, jv, and freshman teams and being one of the top overall programs in Northern California. In the late 1960s we had our first Nor Cal Champion, and by 1974, a CIF State Finalist in Victor Henderson.

It has been just over two years since my wonderful coach has passed. However, it has taken me this long to honor the greatest coach a boy could have had. Coach Lee was the greatest man I ever knew.

All Worth It!
Tuesday, January 29, 2008   10:28 PM

In my years as a high school wrestling coach, I have had many memorable moments. So when I watched Bella Vista beat Casa Robles for the league championship tonight, I was really happy for Mike. One thing that he probably did not realize at the moment was that a team usually reflects the personality and character of its coach.

In this match, Bella Vista had any number of ways to lose. One boy (I don't know his name) was on his back practically the whole match. But he never gave up, not even for one second. Had he said, "Oh, to heck with it," and eased up a LITTLE bit, he would have been pinned. As it was, he gave up 5 team points, but not 6. That kind of heart is not easily learned. Several other of the BV kids could just as easily have lost as won, but BV won all the close ones.

A win like that is what makes coaching young men worthwhile. It certainly is not the money or fame. I can speak with some authority on Mike, having known him and coached him. He is a person of the highest integrity and "never give up" attitude, and his wrestlers reflected those traits. The BV kids won the matches they were supposed to win and battled hard in the ones they lost. That was a true team victory. The wrestlers do not realize it now, but they will remember that win as long as they live. So will the coach!

The Rebirth of a Program
Written by Mike Lee in January of 2010
Mike Lee (no relation) wrestled for Charlie from 1979-1982. He has been the head coach at Bella Vista since 1994.

In the 1980s Bella Vista wrestling was a dominant program. The team placed second in the state three years in a row (1981-1983), won five section championships, produced five individual state champions, one of whom is considered the greatest wrestler in Sacramento history in David Lee, had a coach named National Coach of the Year by Scholastic Magazine (Charlie Lee), and three members of the Lee family would go on to be inducted into the California Wrestling Hall of Fame (Charlie, Ralphene, and David).

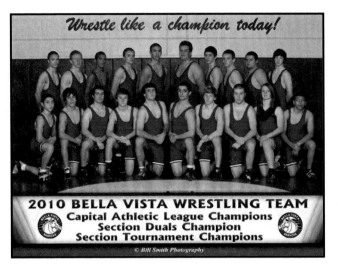

Then the shoe dropped. Charlie retired, and not long after that San Juan Unified School District dropped junior high athletics. Within seven years of being second in the state of California, Bella Vista had 14 total kids on the team, and only two had wrestled before high school.

I took over the program at that point. My name is Mike Lee (not related, but I did wrestle for Charlie) and I am a teacher and wrestling coach at BV. After years of work, Bella Vista wrestling this year is ranked #13 in the state (no divisions, that's every high school, big or small) and we have a wrestler (Jake Briggs) who is ranked #1 in the state at 140 lbs. When I first took over the program, we didn't have a hint of any wrestler qualifying for the state championships. Down the road, we started to send one, then two, three, four, and this year we have a real chance to send six kids to state. We have a well-developed youth program led by Mark Tucker. Those kids get passed on to Dana Smith at the junior high, who does a great job, then up to the high school level. The only reason we have come back is by building a program and having the right people to lead it at the various levels. The original program was built by Charlie and the

Sacramento Super Stars Youth Wrestling Team. Those kids grew into future state champions and medalists. This rebirth was built on our California Xtreme Youth Team, and those kids are now in high school and winning medals at state. While Jake Briggs may be the next state champion, the next David Lee may be our freshman Shayne Tucker. Shayne is a freshman, and he has already beaten a returning state finalist (Stephen Knoblock) and Shayne is currently ranked #8 in the state at 112 lbs. Shayne has also been published in WIN Magazine as one of the top wrestlers in the country—as a freshman.

I thought this to be an interesting story about a very proud program, which fell off the map for wrestling, and is now back in the mix as a top program.

State Meet Memories
By Ralphene

In 2009, Charlie and I were asked by our good friend, Lynn Dyche, to lead a group of wrestlers onto the stage before the finals at the California State Wrestling Tournament held in Bakersfield. We had not attended the state meet in its entirety since David won his third title as a senior in 1984. Charlie's Parkinson's had progressed to the point where his mobility was affected. This was such a moving event for me, I felt I should try to record my thoughts of that evening. I did not realize that doing this would take me back through our family's long wrestling career. These are my reflections, as I recalled them in March of 2009.

To me, wrestling is the toughest sport of all. Wrestlers are a unique breed. True wrestling fans are unique as well. I can't begin to recount all the wrestling memories that Charles and I have shared throughout the years, but here are some of my thoughts, prompted by last weekend's California State Wrestling Championships.

To begin with, California has one state champion in each weight class, unlike every other state in the U.S., with the exception of New York. When a boy is a champion in another state at 145 pounds, there is a 145-pound champ in division one, division two, division three, and so forth. Not in California. If you are the champ at 145, you are THE STATE CHAMP. Californians are quite proud of this format. Due to the sheer size of our state, our masters tournaments (state qualifiers) are quite often larger than most state championships.

Charlie and I had not been to the state championships to experience the entire tournament since 1984 when David won his third title. We had been to the final session twice during those years, first when David was a Hall of Fame inductee, and again when Charles was selected as a member of this prestigious group. We had forgotten what an awesome experience the entire two-day event really is.

Forty-man brackets, six wins in two days—a daunting task at this level. Bella Vista took four young men to state this year, a very good showing. We felt like we truly knew each wrestler, Charlie having worked with them throughout the season, analyzing tapes, talking strategy in our living room.

At the state tournament you will find three groups of wrestlers. There are those who are thrilled to death to qualify for the state meet. It is what they have always dreamed about. Just to say, "I wrestled in the California State Wrestling Tournament" is the ultimate goal for these boys.

The next group are those who have set their sights on a medal. They are not content just to BE there. They want to be on that victory stand.

Then, of course, there is that elite group of wrestlers who have only one thing in mind—the top of the podium. These athletes have trained for years for this event. Most have impressive credentials from many tournaments, but this gold medal is the ultimate. Nothing less will do. Only fourteen athletes will achieve this goal each year. Blood, sweat, and tears define our sport.

Following our four BV wrestlers in their quest this year, first there was Grant, our young sophomore, a very experienced wrestler in his own right. Grant's toughest battle, perhaps, was making the 103-pound weight in which he competed at the end of the season. He needed to drop to 103 because of Bryden, a senior, who dropped to the 112-pound spot. (I could tell some stories here. An awesome young wrestler, Wesley Gaston, pushed out of the lineup for tournament action when Scott Kitchen dropped to the 95-pound division. Two years later, Tracy Yeates, undefeated at 95, number one in the area rankings, knocked out when John Loomis dropped at the end of the year. These are just two cases that come to mind.) The 103-pound weight was so difficult for Grant to make, that he shared his frustration with his friend Jake. The Briggs family immediately pitched in to help ease a difficult situation. They invited Grant to live at their home, where the dieting would be easier for him than in his own home where he had two older brothers who certainly were not dieting. Not many families would work out a situation like this, and my hat goes off to both. This turned out to last for three weeks, since Grant won the league, won the divisional, and then qualified for the state tournament by placing seventh at the masters. Quite an accomplishment for a sophomore. Grant lost his first match at state, being paired against a very short, squatty wrestler, making a difficult match-up for the lanky young man. Dropping to the consolation bracket, Grant was leading 4-0 with just seconds to go in the match, riding his opponent, when he hung his head, and was reversed to his back, losing 5-4 as the towel came in—a match he will long remember. Hopefully, it will be a motivator that will carry Grant to a medal next year.

Bruce, a senior, had an extremely successful season. We had learned Bruce's story just a few days before the state meet. When he began wrestling in middle school, he lost almost every match. He was not discouraged, however, and kept coming back for more and working harder still in the practice room, gradually improving as time went on. Who would have guessed that, as a senior, this young man would qualify for the state meet AND win two matches there. Bruce's matches were won on heart and desire. It is wrestlers like Bruce that make wrestling the awesome sport that it is.

Next comes Bryden, a shy senior now wrestling at 112 after competing at 119 for the early part of the season. Bryden's high school record was in the ballpark of 150 wins and 28 losses going into the state meet. He had been in the top twelve at state as a junior. At this year's tournament, Bryden won several matches, but came up short in his bid for a state medal. After the 3-2 loss that eliminated him from competition, he took off his wrestling shoes and left them on the mat. Any wrestling fan knows what that means. The good news is that Bryden petitioned into the Senior National Tournament to be held in early April in Virginia and will be wrestling there. We are hopeful that he will find the perfect collegiate situation, if he chooses to go on.

Then there is Jake. Jake won the masters tournament as a freshman and placed fourth at state that year. An amazing accomplishment, especially in the state of California. His sophomore year he failed to medal. He is a junior this year and has been working extremely hard all season with one thing in mind. He has spent many evenings in our living room, looking at tapes and talking wrestling with Charlie. We have watched his confidence grow by leaps and bounds. He is not the same wrestler he was last year at this time. Jake wrestled an awesome state tournament. He won his first three matches, then lost by a score of 8-6 to the eventual champion, Henry Yorba of Poway. Being the true competitor that he is, Jake bounced back and won his next four bouts to place third. He was the only junior in a field of eight medalists, all the others seniors. We hope to be in the audience to watch Jake finish the job next year!

Young Bella Vista wrestlers Bruce Pfau, Grant Burkhalter, Jake Briggs, and Bryden Lazaro at Coach Lee's Memorial Service on December 28, 2010.

Watching these young men compete brings so many other memories to mind. The young freshman phenom, Alex Cisneros, who walked through the 103-pound division so easily this year. Some people say he is certain to be the second four-timer in California history. Believe me, the Lee family knows that this may be easier said than done. As Charlie has always said, the wrestling is just one part. There are so many OTHER ways to lose a state title. I wish Alex luck. California needs another four-time champion.

Vlad Dombrowski, the young man from the Ukraine who took the wrestling community by surprise last year by winning the 140-pound state title. As defending champion this year, he was pinned in his semi-final match, with one second remaining in the second period. What a disappointment. He accepted his loss with the grace of a true champion and fought back valiantly to place third.

And now we come to the state champions. Our first was Lynn Mason. Lynn was a tough 165-pounder his senior year (1967). He wrestled his state final literally one-armed, with a broken collarbone, but with the courage of a champion, he won.

Our next champ was Mark Loomis, John's older brother. (The Loomis brothers should have attended Mira Loma. The number of athletes who moved to the BV area to wrestle for Charlie is another story to be told.) Charlie always said that Mark was the laziest wrestler he ever coached in the practice-room. But put him on the mat in competition, and look out!

After Mark came Tracy Yeates. Tracy won the state title his junior year. David was a freshman, and had failed to qualify for the state meet. I remember thinking, as I watched the introductions of the finalists and Tracy's final match, that if my son EVER won a state title I would be the happiest mom alive. Who would have dreamed it would happen the very next year?

That brings us to the state meet in 1982. David was a sophomore and was entering the state meet with just one loss, an overtime loss in the finals of the Coast Classic to Durbin Lloren, a good friend of his from Tracy, who later that year became a state champion himself. David had defeated Cordova's Jeff Hazzard by a score of 2-1 in the finals of the section the week before state. Hazzard was a blue-chip recruit for Coach Chris Horpel of Stanford, and that recalls another very funny experience that my daughter and I share—a story I would title, "My Brother is a Wrestler." (Maybe someday.)

David had wrestled an outstanding tournament, defeating Brian Folsom of Southern California by one point in the semis.

A convincing one-point victory, but one point, nevertheless. Would you believe that Brian's father Rod had approached Charlie a few years earlier about moving his family to Fair Oaks for Brian to wrestle at BV, having seen the success of the Sacramento Super Stars? Mr. Folsom's comment was, "I am a brick layer and I can lay bricks in Sacramento as well as I can in LA!" He went so far as to fly a small plane to Phoenix Field and look for a house for his family. I'm not sure why that move never happened. I kind of think Mrs. Folsom might have had a say in the decision. It might have been tough for Brian to make our team!

Kind of a tradition at the state meet, at least in our day, was that people just hung out between the medal rounds and time for the doors to open for the finals at six. Quite often these were lovely spring days and people gathered on the grass in front of the high school or at some nearby pizza parlor. Of course wrestling dominated the conversation. Talk of the finals, the medalists, which section was toughest, etc.—such fun to share wrestling talk with fans and friends from all over the state. I distinctly remember sitting on a grassy hillside before the doors opened for the finals in David's sophomore year. I was visiting with some wrestling friends from the valley, and Mrs. Dennington, Brandon's mom, asked me if I was nervous and how I was feeling, with such an important match looming ahead for David. (Brandon and David had grown up as good friends through kid wrestling programs, although David was older than Brandon.) Was I nervous? Oh yeah! I could hardly sit still, but it helped to talk to friends. Strangely enough, just a few years later (I am not sure how many) Mrs. Dennington found herself in the exact situation. Brandon, as a sophomore, had qualified for the finals. Their result was not as happy as ours, because Brandon lost in the finals that year. However, he came back to win it the next two years, becoming a two-time state champ.

The pageantry, the introductions—I hardly remember any of that. I do remember that when David was called for his match, I went up to the very top tier of seats and leaned on the balcony railing to watch the match away from the crowd. I could NOT sit still. Fortunately, our good friend Frank Berry found his way up to stand beside me. David was wrestling Jeff Tripp, a fine wrestler from Yucaipa. All started well, and David had a 2-1 lead at the end of the first period. Then the fireworks started. Tripp was in the up position and early in the period, managed to cradle David. For 45 seconds, give or take a few, David found himself in a position he was unfamiliar with. He was on his back and in danger of being pinned. The referee laid on his stomach, looking right at David's shoulders, and signaled with his hand that there was just an inch to go. This seemed to go on forever. To be honest, I thought it was lights out. I hid behind Frank with my head buried in his shoulder and he kept me apprised of what was going on. I could not watch. Finally David managed to free himself, and then the fun began. I can't recall the exact details of the rest of the match, but David had the composure to let Tripp up twice and take him down each time to secure the win. And what a win that was for him, setting the stage for the possibility of California's first three-time state champ. Teammate Tracy Yeates, who had won it all the year before, had to settle for fourth place that year. It is TOUGH to win that tournament more than once.

In our home, from the spring of 1982 to the state tourney in 1984, I do not ever recall Charlie, or David, or myself discussing the possibility of him winning three championships. Yes, it was certainly on our minds, but it was not something we discussed. It didn't drastically change our lives. Reporters, fans, and friends would continually bring up the subject, and of course we discussed it with them, but we did not talk about it at home. We didn't need to—we all felt the same. In the same vein, the win did not change David's workout routine or match preparation or lifestyle. He continued to take each match one at a time, as he had always done. And I am very proud to say, he continued to be the modest young wrestler he had always been.

David's junior year was fun. That year David was joined at the top of the podium by good friend and teammate, Ken Gaudreau. Kenny won the state title at 103 pounds. Kenny was always a hard worker, as well as a team leader, and we were so happy for him and for his family.

In August of David's senior year, he came running into the house one day, exclaiming that he was heading out for football practice! I was shocked, and not exactly thrilled. Football had always been a passion of David's. I remember John Loomis and him playing many hours with the electric football field that moved the small players around. David had played football as a freshman, and was a darn good lineman. He gave it up the next two years to concentrate on wrestling. That August day I asked him if he had checked with his dad about his decision to play, and he said, "Yes, he said if I love the game and want to play, go for it!" I could just see that third title flying out the window! Once again, David was coached by his dad. BV had a great team that year, playing in the city and section championships. David was selected as an all-conference guard. I am very glad he had that experience.

David's senior year was simply a matter of how long a wrestler could last on the mat with him. He ended the season with a record of 50-0, 46 wins by fall. I am not sure how many opponents David pinned before a wrestler lasted the full six minutes. I believe it was somewhere in the high 30s, but I am not sure. The *Sacramento Bee* ran a big headline saying, "Lee's Pin Streak Ends!" One would have thought that he had lost a match, if they did not read carefully.

It was a pleasure to watch David during his senior year. He was truly an athlete at the top of his game. Of course the possibility of being California's first three-time state champ hung over him wherever he went. At the state meet, after defeating his final opponent from Clovis West by a decisive score, David's only display of emotion was a small fist pump to himself as he looked up at the crowd. Then into his dad's waiting embrace. What a moment! During the awards ceremony, after David's weight class was presented with their medals, the ceremony was stopped, and a special presentation was made. A group of state officials had prepared a special plaque, proclaiming David as the first three-time California State Champ. There were a lot of pictures taken, and quite a fuss made over this special event. Charlie later asked the friend who had originated the idea for this award, what he would have done if David had not won the title. The friend's answer was, "I had no fear of that happening, but if it had, I guess I would have just taken the plaque down and thrown it in the river!" Kenny Gaudreau placed fourth that year, after his win as a junior. It is tough to win that title more than once!

Bella Vista had one state champion after David. Tony Kitchen, one of the youngest of our Super Star Wrestling Club, won the title his senior year. Charlie and I still laugh at our favorite story of Tony's childhood years. He was a feisty little kid who won almost every match he wrestled. In fact, after the first match he lost (I believe Betty said he was five at the time) he tried to flush his wrestling shoes down the toilet. He was not going to wrestle anymore!

Back to the 2009 State Tournament. It was great to see so many dear friends whom we had not seen for many years. Lynn Dyche, "Mr. California Wrestling" in my book, is the guy who makes the tournament the incredible success that it is. Sandy Stevens is the best announcer in the business. (Along with good friend, Ed Aliverti, of course.) Sandy and I have worked dozens of wrestling tournaments together at the national level. She is a true professional in every sense of the word, and to hear her voice welcome the crowd to our state meet brought tears to my eyes. Duane Morgan, such a good friend for many years, who has done so much for our wonderful sport. Monty Muller working in an important official position, evaluating and coordinating the officiating. Bill Grant, who has done so much for this sport for so many years, much of it behind the scenes, with little or no recognition. Throughout the tournament many people came up to shake Charlie's hand and to chat. Many whose faces were familiar, but whose names I no longer recall. All good friends through the sport of wrestling.

Charlie and I had been asked by Lynn Dyche to lead a group of medalists to the stage in the Parade of Champions. Many of the inductees for this year's Hall of Fame group would be participating in the parade, along with other Hall of Fame members. On Friday, Lynn showed me what this would involve. We were to assemble with the other presenters in the tunnel, and when our group was called, we would walk down one side of the huge Rabobank Arena, around the end, up the other side, then across to the elevated stage that had been constructed to hold the lone mat for the finals. Then up eight steep stairs to the mat. Charlie and I talked about how this might work for him, knowing Mr. Parkinson might play a part in our final decision. Dealing with Parkinson's for nineteen years, as we have done, we know that it is not possible to predict how Charlie will be able to function at any particular time. Nights are usually the worst, when his medication has worn off. We decided we had three options. To use his scooter, to use the walker, or to walk together. We also knew that this decision might have to change at the very last moment.

Both of us were very nervous about this adventure, but excited too, and very proud to be asked to participate. We left for the arena very early, needing to get the scooter or walker downstairs through security and to the staging area. At the head table area we encountered several of the newly-selected Hall of Fame inductees. Longtime friend/rival coach Bill Flake of Placer High School was there. Of course he and Charlie recounted memorable matches through the years and also traded fishing stories. Max Burch, a good friend from Redding, was there as well. Max had two boys who were several years older than David, and we all shared many good times. Richard Fox, coach of the awesome Ponderosa dynasty that followed on the heels of Bella Vista's success, was there as well. Richard has always said that he patterned his program after ours. A huge compliment, I believe. Charlie also visited with many coaches whom I did not know personally, although I recognized most of the faces.

At 6 pm, the group was asked to move to the staging area under the arena and line up in order. We were to lead the group of 135-pound medalists. We all moved into place, and the evening's festivities began. While we were held backstage, many introductions were made, California wrestling history presented, etc. All this took a long while, and we were still grappling with the problem of how Charlie should make the long trek. If he sat on the scooter backstage to rest, he ran the risk of freezing up, but if he stood all that time, he would become so tired he might not be able to make the walk, if that is what he decided to do. The group presented just before the competitors was the officials. Kenny Gaudreau was among that group. Ken has established himself as one of the best young officials in the state, and we are so proud to watch him on the mat. Cody Olson is another of our alums who referees. Cody refs on a national level, having officiated a final match at the

NCAAs very recently. These young men include Charlie in their occasional poker games, and he certainly enjoys that.

By now we were in the tunnel, and I could hear Sandy's voice saying something to the effect of, "And now, ladies and gentlemen, I present to you the finest young wrestlers in the United States of America." Her voice, even when I hear her on television, has always given me goose bumps. As always, this whole ceremony was carefully crafted, and each group was held for a few minutes to give Sandy time to speak of the Hall of Fame member leading each specific weight class. I wish I could have been sitting in the audience to hear her exact words as the various weight divisions filed in. When we came out of the tunnel the arena was completely dark, except for the spotlights lighting the stage and the contestants. Charlie had decided to walk for this important event (I always knew that would be his decision). The two of us started out side by side, and what an experience it was to see the thousands of people in that arena, all standing and cheering loudly as the various groups came by. As we walked slowly the length of the arena, I could hardly see through a mist of tears. I saw faces, I saw waves, I saw salutes, I saw so many, many smiles and nods of acknowledgement. Perhaps the thing that touched me most was a group of three ladies standing together, all blowing kisses to us. I know that I must have worked many tournaments with those wonderful ladies, in pairing rooms somewhere along the line. I only wish that I had had time to visit with them and thank them. They made me realize that in that crowd of thousands, there must be many many more people whom Charlie and I had worked with throughout our years of wrestling. That realization almost overwhelmed me.

After we rounded the far end of the arena we came in front of the Bella Vista rooting section. In the huge crowd the first person I spotted was Mike Lee, broad smile on his face, arms upraised. I know Mike was feeling proud of his old coach. I know he was feeling proud to have once wrestled for BV, and I am sure he was feeling extremely proud to be the coach of the Bella Vista wrestling program now. We had so many loyal fans in that audience. I think I briefly glimpsed each one of them, but one who I will never forget is John Briggs, Jake's grandfather, a Vietnam War veteran. John Briggs makes Charlie look small! He and Charlie sit together at most tournaments in two large chairs, front row and center.

They make quite a formidable pair! Mr. Briggs has always been so respectful of Charlie and makes comments about Charlie owning the gym, being able to sit in the center of the mat if he wished, and the wrestlers would just wrestle around him. I think he might be Charlie's number-one fan. And there he was, looming tall in the front row, arms pumping as he chanted so proudly, "That's our coach! That's our coach!" It was hard to hold back the tears.

We turned the corner for the walk across the arena to the stage. This was the part we were unsure of. Those eight steps looked so steep, and the wait once we reached the top would seem interminable. We had talked with Lynn about the possibility of Charlie standing below, at the foot of the stairs, but one sidelong glance at him and I knew that wasn't going to happen. We approached the stairs and I went up first, Charlie right behind me. Once we were together at the top of the stairs, we started across the mat. And there, out of the blue, was a familiar face. Rulon Gardner! Some of you have heard or read my account of the young wrestler who was 22 seconds late to weigh-ins for the Olympic Trials in 1992 and was eliminated from the competition. That was Rulon as a young college wrestler, virtually unknown at the time. He made history in Sydney in 2000 by defeating the Russian phenom, Alexander Karelin, 1-0 in the heavyweight finals. Karelin had never lost a match in international competition to that point, and it was the final match of his career. To see him leave his shoes on the mat was truly heartbreaking. (We had personally followed his career ever since we first met him at the 1987 Espoir tournament in Colorado Springs, in which David also competed. We would see him through many years of competing at the Concord International.) Rulon had been brought in as a celebrity draw and had an autograph session on Saturday that had hundreds of people standing in line to get his signature. I do not know him personally, but we know each other through our roles in the sport of wrestling, and there he was with a smile and a wink just for me, guiding us to our position with the others on the stage.

The other weight groups filed in one by one, each group making the march around the huge arena, then onto the stage. When all were in, Rulon addressed the audience, recognizing the magnitude of our great state meet. Sandy concluded the ceremonial part, and then it was time for the National Anthem. Another connection—

the Star Spangled Banner was sung by a former state champ, Mel East, whom John Loomis used to compete with at the state level.

Finally the presentations were over, and the groups filed off the stage. I had watched Charlie throughout, knowing how tired he was, and wondering how he could possibly continue to stand straight and tall, but he did. We made our way back under the arena and then to our seats to watch the finals.

It was a privilege to be on the same stage with those outstanding young men. (Jake made the comment to Charlie, "Coach, I never saw you in a suit before!") If a reporter from ESPN had asked me, "Mrs. Lee, how did it feel to be on the stage with so many talented wrestlers?" I am sure I would have used every superlative in the book. It was awesome, it was exciting, it was an honor, and on and on. I can tell you this—I did not mind one bit being the only female up there! When I realize, as I often do, what an honor it is to be the only woman inducted thus far into this elite Hall of Fame group, so many thoughts run through my mind. There are many women in the state more deserving than I. I only hope my presence represents each one of them.

I know that last weekend reaffirmed my love and appreciation for the sport of wrestling. There was one man on that stage Saturday night who showed as much courage and heart as any competitor in those finals. In my daughter's words, "Mom, Dad deserved the biggest medal of all." I have NEVER been more proud of my husband.

Bella Vista Wrestlers: David Call, Bruce Pfau, Grant Burkhalter, Landon Burkhalter, Jacob Kern, and Josh Lazaro at Coach Lee's Memorial Service.

Wrestling

Team Captain Dillon Mueller designed this head gear logo for the 2010 team in remembrance of Coach Lee.

Victor Trujillo and Grandfather, David, at Bella Vista's 2013 Senior Night. Victor's many honors include being a two-time California state medalist and a High School All-American. Vic is a sophomore and a second-year starter for Cal Poly San Luis Obispo.

Family support has long been a trademark of the BV wrestling program. Senior wrestlers Victor Trujillo, Sam Fowler, Shayne Tucker, Preston Layton, and Justin Calderon shown here with their parents at the 2013 Senior Night ceremony.

The 2013 Bella Vista team is shown here after winning the Sac-Joaquin Division II Section Championships. Charlie's granddaughter, Alex Stadnik (shown at right), was strength and conditioning coach for the team while living with Ralphene and completing her master's thesis in Sports Conditioning and Performance.

Jennifer Page is a 2011 Bella Vista graduate. Her father, Garth Page, wrestled for Charlie in the 1970s. At Bella Vista, Jennifer won 55 varsity matches and was a three-time section medalist (all against boys). She attended the 2012 Olympic Games in London as an alternate on the U.S. Women's team and is currently the #2 ranked U.S. wrestler at her weight.

Coach Mike Lee called Alex Bluemel the "next in line to add his name to the greats of Bella Vista wrestling." Alex qualified for the California State Tournament in both 2014 and 2015.

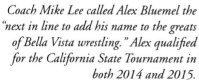

Wrestling

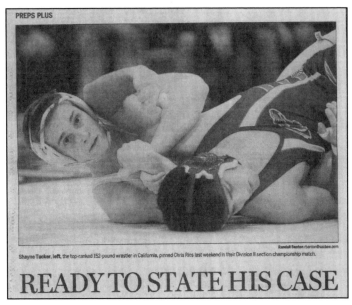

Randall Benton rbenton@sacbee.com

Shayne Tucker, left, the top-ranked 152-pound wrestler in California, pinned Chris Rios last weekend in their Division II section championship match.

READY TO STATE HIS CASE

2013 Bella Vista graduate Shayne Tucker. Shayne had an outstanding high school career, placing fourth at the state meet as a sophomore, and second in his junior and senior years. Shayne's overall high school record was 184-26. In 2014 Shayne started for Oklahoma University as a redshirt freshman. He is the 2015 Big 12 Conference Champion at 149 pounds.

Charlie Lee
Bella Vista Coach
1962-1984

Mike Lee
Bella Vista Coach
1994-Present

**Charlie and Mike are not related but
remained close friends throughout the years.**

Certain teams are pictured throughout the book, usually in connection with a particular story. However, each of Charlie's wrestlers, and each of his teams, was very special to him. This collection completes the 22 teams that Charlie coached throughout the years.

1964 BV Wrestling Team

1966 BV Wrestling Team

1967 BV Wrestling Team

1968 BV Wrestling Team

1969 BV Wrestling Team

1971 BV Wrestling Team

1972 BV Wrestling Team

1974 BV Wrestling Team

1975 BV Wrestling Team

1977 BV Wrestling Team

1978 BV Wrestling Team

Wrestling

1980 BV Wrestling Team

1982 BV Wrestling Team

FOOTBALL

Football
By Ralphene

Little did Charlie and I know while we were going to school at the University of Iowa that the football team would be one of the most successful and revered in the history of the school. Charlie's five years playing for the Hawkeyes were literally the stuff of which dreams are made. Two Rose Bowl Championships, three Big Ten Championships, participating as a senior in the 1960 Copper Bowl, the All-American Bowl, and the 1961 Hula Bowl, and a team record of 37-8-2 during his career—not many athletes have such an opportunity. We were "living the dream" and didn't even realize it!

Headlines from Des Moines Register *sports pages for 1960 Hawkeye Football season.*

Coach Forest Evashevski

*Charlie's media shot
for the Iowa Hawkeyes
in 1958.*

My Life in Football

I began my football life at El Camino High School in my freshman year. The coach was Ray Schultz. He cut me from the team for missing a practice without an excuse. I was later to be his assistant at Bella Vista in my first year as a teacher and coach, kind of ironic. When our family moved to Fair Oaks, I enrolled in San Juan High School where I played jv as a sophomore, and then varsity my junior and senior years. I was all-league my senior year, which I thought was a big deal, but it really meant very little in light of what I was about to jump into.

My history teacher, Joe Murtaugh, somehow took a liking to me and said to my dad that he thought he might be able to get me some kind of football scholarship at the University of Iowa. He said he had quite a few connections at several Big Ten schools. We thought he was just talking hot air, but it turned out he knew what he was doing. On the strength of his recommendation alone, I received a full scholarship offer from Iowa. This was at a time when there were no films to look at, and being from California, no scout from Iowa had seen me play.

I also had football offers from the University of California at Berkeley and the Air Force Academy. If I had chosen Air Force, I would have had to spend my first year at a prep school in Roswell, New Mexico in order to bring my grades up to their admission standards. Air Force was really never a serious consideration since I hated the thought of flying.

I had an offer from the Pittsburgh Pirates baseball club to sign a contract (this was right out of high school) and they offered me a $3,000 signing bonus. I loved baseball and was really tempted to take their offer. $3,000 was a lot of money in 1956—you could buy a new car with that kind of money. My parents put a quick kibosh on that idea, so it was off to Iowa for me.

I remember leaving from the train station in downtown Sacramento. My dad and mom and my grandparents, Wally and Marie Young, and my brother Bruce were on hand to see me off. I was just 17 years old and about to get a rude awakening in regards to being an all-league high school football player versus a Big Ten football player. I thought I was pretty hot stuff since I had no trouble handling the high school kids I played against.

I got off the train in Iowa City with no one to meet me, 17 years old, and one suitcase in hand. I had been told in a letter to report to the field house when I got to Iowa City. I didn't know what a field house was! I got in a cab and said, "Take me to the field house." The driver proceeded to drive me to the field house, which was a large athletic complex next to the football stadium. I was told to look up the freshman football coach whose name was Jerry Hilgenberg. When I walked into the field house, there must have been 30 or 40 other young men standing around or sitting against the walls. As it turned out, we were all freshman football players. After a lot of sitting around and some confusion, Coach Hilgenberg and some assistants appeared and finally figured out who everyone was, and we got shuffled off to our rooms at the dorm. It seemed to me at the time to be kind of unorganized, and I didn't know what I was doing. This was two weeks before the start of classes. It was the time the football staff got to know everyone. Freshmen were not allowed to compete at the varsity level at that time, and we played no games.

There was no limit on the number of football scholarships that a university could give at that time. There were 105 freshmen in my class, each on some form of scholarship. That is a huge number. Today that number is limited to 30 a year. Several years after I graduated, I returned and talked to Bob Flora, the line coach. I asked him what he thought caused the decline of the quality of football in the Big Ten. He said, at least as he knew it at Iowa, they upped the admission requirements and cut back the number of scholarships. But I am getting ahead of myself.

There were 17 people out for the position of freshman tackle. One thing that really appealed to me was that after we checked into the dorm on that first day, we were given a food card to the cafeteria, which meant we could eat as much as we wanted for nothing. I remember how great it was to drink five cartons of milk and pay nothing for it. After we had signed up for classes and school began, we could go to the university book store and pick out any and all books we wanted, no charge. You can imagine how this opened up room for considerable abuse. A player could go buy a brand-new medical book that cost $200 and turn it back in for $100 cash. This practice was not uncommon. Of the 105 freshmen that comprised my freshman class, only five of us received our degrees.

At that time there was no platoon system in effect, which meant a player would have to go both ways, offense and defense. There were a great many players on that freshman team. One particular guy from Hackensack, New Jersey, also at the tackle position, was a fantastic defensive football player. I would say as good as Alex Karras, who was the Outland Trophy Winner that year for the outstanding lineman in the country. However, this kid could not remember the plays on offense, so he did not play. He dropped out of school before the year was over, as did many others.

One factor that I think determined my success at Iowa in football was that I never missed a single practice, and I hardly ever made a mistake on offense (blocking assignments, etc.). Coach Evashevski was a real stickler for that. My freshman year, Iowa went to the Rose Bowl for the first time in years and defeated Oregon State by a score of 35-19. Oddly enough, the two teams had played the opening game of the season and Iowa won that game by one point.

Teammates getting ready to board the plane to California for the 1959 Rose Bowl. Front row: Dick Clark, John Leshyn, Al Dunn. Back Row: Charlie Lee, Al Sonnenberg.

At the start of my sophomore year, I was probably fifth or sixth team. I was given number 99, and my name did not even appear in the program. There were two 99s. The other player was better than I was, and his name was listed in the program. As the year progressed, the coaches seemed to take more notice of me. I remember at one film-viewing session of a scrimmage, Evashevski stopped the film and pointed out one outstanding block I had made. This was a very unusual thing for him to do. A few days later when we scrimmaged again, I was placed on the third team, ahead of a fellow named Bill Scott, a big 6 ft. 7 in. guy who I was battling with for that position. That weekend, we were playing Ohio State in Columbus on Saturday. On Friday, I received a call from Bob Flora, our head line coach, who told me I was going to be flying with him and Archie Kodros, the other line coach, to Columbus. I was thrilled, and I suited up for the game and even played some. We lost that game, and on our return to Iowa City, at the next week's practice, I noticed my name was listed as officially the third-team tackle, which meant I qualified for training table. This was a HUGE deal. As the season progressed, I made all the road trips and played in several games. I was always announced by the other number 99's name, so officially, I did not play that year, which as it turned out, was quite a good thing for me.

At the start of my junior year, I made the second team, which meant I saw a lot of playing time. On the bus traveling to the Minnesota game, Bob Flora sat down next to me and told me that at the first of the month, I should go to Towner's Department Store (a high class women's clothing store) and they might have some work for me. I did this, and come to find out, this was to be my sponsor. All guys on the first two teams had sponsors. In my case, I was supposedly stacking boxes and cleaning up, for which they paid me $200 a month. I wonder what Bobby Jeter or Alex Karras or Randy Duncan were getting! That year we were Big Ten Champions, and ended up the season being #1 in the rankings by one poll, and LSU was ranked #1 in the other poll. We beat Cal in the Rose Bowl by a score of 38-12. (It could have been 60-0.) They were the worst team we played all year.

At the Rose Bowl we had two players to a room at the Beverly Hilton Hotel, and each pair shared a brand-new 1960 Oldsmobile, gassed up every morning. Evashevski gave us a lot of free time to really enjoy ourselves, and we did. We were treated like royalty. At some bowl games the following year, I talked to players from Ohio State who had gone to the Rose Bowl under Woody Hayes. They said they hated the experience. It was like military boot camp. No free time, short curfew hours, lots of live practice—not a great memory. In our case, come game time we were ready to play football.

Evashevski, who was a real stickler for promptness, always insisted on leaving on time, whether it was by plane, bus, or train. The morning of the game we were all on the bus. Archie Kodros read off the names, and we responded by saying, "Here." Everyone was present with the exception of Mark Manders. He was my best friend, an All-American guard, and scheduled to see a lot of action in the game. Evy looked at his watch and said, "Let's go." When Mark came to the lobby a few minutes later, the bus was gone. As it turned out, he got to the coliseum on the back seat of a motorcycle cop. He played a lot, but he never missed the bus again!

My senior year, academically, I was first team starting tackle and enjoyed a very successful season. During the summer between my fourth and fifth years, I attended summer school to take a course in physiology that I had flunked, mainly because I was taking it with all pre-med students, and they graded on a straight curve and I was not up to their academic standards. At summer school I received a B, with the help of one of Ralphene's best friends, Nancy Noll. I can remember at one point that summer, I was so poor I did not have a nickel to my name. The only thing to eat in the house where I was staying with some other players was a one-gallon can of tomatoes. At the end of summer school, Bob Flora called me in and asked me if I would show a couple of high school recruits around. I said sure. He gave me cart blanche to the Big Ten Inn, and a card that gave me unlimited expenses at the student union— food and games, bowling, pool, etc. I remember getting ahold of Mark Manders, who was living in a trailer park with his wife, and taking him and the high school kids on a tour of the campus. We spent a lot of time at the student union and finished with a great meal at the Big Ten Inn, which I really could use, courtesy of the athletic department. I never returned the student union card to Flora, because he never asked me for it. I did not abuse it, but I certainly did take advantage of it my whole senior year! I did a lot of bowling, shot a lot of pool, had all the great meals I wanted, courtesy of that card. The subject of the card never came up.

However, because I *officially* did not play my sophomore year, I had one year of eligibility left, so I came back on full scholarship as starting left tackle. We were Co-Big Ten Champions with Minnesota that year. We did not go to the Rose Bowl because Minnesota had beaten us in head-to-head competition. They beat us, Ohio State beat them, and we beat Ohio State.

Ralphene and I had planned a June wedding when we graduated, but when I was chosen to play in three post-season bowl games, the Copper Bowl in Phoenix, Arizona, the All-American Bowl in Tucson, and the Hula Bowl in Honolulu, it seemed like too good an opportunity to pass up as a honeymoon—all expenses paid! At all the bowl games, if you brought your wife, she came free. If you did not bring a wife, they gave you a certain amount of money. Imagine the Wards' surprise when we made a phone call in late

November saying we planned to move our wedding date from June to sometime in early December! This meant Nina, Ralphene's mom, now had approximately two weeks to put the wedding together! We selected December 10th as our wedding date. Would you believe that our wedding colors were black and gold? When Ralph received the measurements of the groomsmen sent by me, he went to the town's tailor shop, owned by Jim O'Connor, president of the Mt. Pleasant HS Boosters' Club. He gave Jim the measurements, and Jim's comment was, "My God, Ralph, this looks like the whole Iowa line!" My future father-in-law quickly assured him that that was exactly what it was. Jim had to send to Des Moines for tuxes to fit the group! The entire wedding went off without a hitch. On the day we left to fly out, a reporter from the Des Moines Peach section was on hand. A large picture of us was on the front page of the sports section the next day, suitcases in hand. The caption read, "Football Pays for this Honeymoon," followed by a long article.

Ralphene and Charlie with the Copper Bowl team at the Stardust Casino in Las Vegas while on their honeymoon in 1960.

I was drafted by the Houston Oilers of the new American Football Conference, so Ralphene and I flew from Cedar Rapids to Chicago where we boarded a jet—my first experience on a jet—and flew

Football

to Houston. We were met at the airport by a representative of the Houston Oilers and taken to a ritzy hotel. We received first class treatment. That night we were guests of the owner of the Oilers, Bud Adams, at the Banquet for the Bluebonnet Bowl, which was played in Houston. We were wined and dined and treated royally. At one point during the banquet, after the waiters brought in the Flaming Baked Alaska, the lights were turned off and celebrities in attendance were introduced. I remember being introduced as the potential new right guard for the Oilers. I was introduced right after Joe DiMaggio! Heady stuff!! The following morning we went to Bud Adams's office. I had no agent to negotiate my contract. I was overmatched. There was a bevy of lawyers in the office, and I was offered a $2,000 signing bonus and a salary of $8,500 a year. To give you some idea of what that meant, at that time the top teacher's salary in San Juan was $6,000 a year. I signed and took the bonus.

After Houston, we flew to Tucson and Phoenix to those bowl games, and then on to Hawaii for the Hula Bowl. My best friend Mark Manders and his wife Barbara were also there. My team won all three bowl games. Upon our return to Iowa City, we had been gone 31 days and returned with $11 more than when we left. You might say we had a 31-day free honeymoon!

Back in Iowa City we resumed our life in our attic apartment at the Blue Top Motel. After graduation in June, I left Ralphene in Mt. Pleasant and drove to Houston for training camp. I was there a couple weeks, and just before the final cut, decided that this was not the life for me. I think I would have made the team and been one of those hangers-on who gets traded every couple years or so. But I don't think I would have made a top-quality professional football player.

I returned to Mt. Pleasant in August and looked for a teaching job, but at that late date most jobs were filled. I received a call from Bob Hoff, my old master teacher at The University of Iowa, who had just been hired as head football coach at Central Missouri State College in Warrensburg, Missouri. He asked if I would be interested in coming down with him and being his assistant coach and getting my master's degree. Since it was the only offer I had, down we went! They got Ralphene a job teaching kindergarten on

Whiteman Air Force Base just outside town, at $2,800 a year. We struggled through that year, poor as church mice. I received my master's degree in June. I was looking for a teaching and football job and heard of an opening at Elk Grove HS in California. I wrote my old high school principal, George White, and asked him for a recommendation. The next thing I knew, Mr. White, who was on his way back to visit his daughter on the East Coast, stopped in Warrensburg and offered me a teaching job at Bella Vista, the new school where he was principal. The school district had a rule that no one could be hired without a personal interview, which was his reason for stopping in Warrensburg. I was quite lucky to get the job. Full-time PE jobs were highly sought after. I started my coaching career at BVHS as assistant varsity coach to Ray Schultz. It so happened that my younger brother Bruce attended the school. He ended up being the starting quarterback for two years, and I had the pleasure of coaching him.

For the next 32 years I coached football at all levels in high school. When David was a freshman, I moved down to coach the freshman team with my friend Frank Berry. Don Driscoll's son, Tim, was also a freshman, as were Gordon Pistochini's son, Gregg, and Larry Fletcher's son, Brett. The entire football staff had sons on the freshman team at the same time! They were a ball to coach, and the team went undefeated. Many schools accused us of pouring it on, and maybe we did!

Excerpt from
What It Means to Be a Hawkeye
by Lyle Hammes
By Ralphene

In 2010, a young man by the name of Lyle Hammes collaborated on a book about Kirk Ferentz and some of Iowa's greatest players. Charlie was asked to write his personal account of his years playing at Iowa to be included in the book. Material from the former piece about his playing years at Iowa is included in the article, but Charlie concludes his narrative by saying,

"I spent five full years at the University of Iowa, and played four years during the days when freshmen were not eligible. I had the privilege of contributing during one of the most prominent eras of Iowa football history. Forest Evashevski, more than any other person, made Iowa's success possible. He insisted upon excellence, could not accept mental mistakes, and had the respect of every player I ever knew. That's not an easy thing for a football coach. His admonition, "It's no disgrace to lose, but it is the rankest kind of shame to be outfought," inspired me and guided me through many locker room talks of my own during my 32 years of coaching. The memories I have of the Iowa fans cheering for their Hawkeyes as we walked from the Field House to the Stadium on game day, and the pride and support we all felt from those fans linger to this day. When I call myself a Hawkeye, I think not only of the Iowa team, but of the whole state. My grave marker will be at a small cemetery in Mt. Pleasant, Iowa, my wife's hometown, and I intend to have a symbol of the Hawkeyes engraved in the right corner along with the words, 'On Iowa.'"

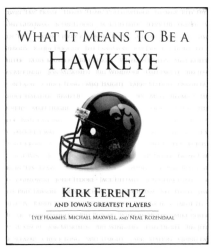

"What It Means To Be A Hawkeye"
includes the story of Charlie's football life
at Iowa.

Surf's Up!

In 1961, when we were in Hawaii for the Hula Bowl, we decided to go surfing. My best friend Mark Manders had also been selected to play in the game. So Ralphene and I, and Mark and his wife Barbara, rented surf boards. None of us had ever surfed before (Iowans???) and we were certainly no good at it. No one got up even once.

We were not paying attention, but we had all been caught in some type of undertow that was taking us toward San Francisco. By the time we realized what was happening, we were a long way from shore. We paddled like crazy, but were making no progress and just getting pooped. We began to shout and wave. It was very unnerving. We were finally spotted by someone on the beach, and this little Hawaiian guy, no more than five feet tall and 120 pounds, comes out on a surfboard that looked like it had a motor. He proceeded to take us, one at a time, back to shore. He would put our surfboard on top of his, and one of us on top of the two boards, then he would get on top of that person and quickly motor us back to shore. He did that four times and wasn't even tired!

That was the last of our surfing adventures! We leave the surfing to David now!

Quack, Quack, Quack!

I have always been an avid hunter—particularly water fowl. In my sophomore year of college I purchased a Browning over/under 12-gauge shotgun. A truly magnificent work of the gun-smith trade. It cost $200, which was a pretty fair amount in 1958.

The starting guard on the football team at the time was a fellow by the name of Gary Grouwinkle from Wapello, Iowa. He also loved to hunt ducks. The Lake Wapello area is famous for its duck and goose hunting. There were several guys on the team who liked to hunt, so Gary would make arrangements for some of the players to go to Wapello on Sundays after our Saturday games. We were surprised by the treatment we received. When we arrived (about an hour before daylight) we were always treated to an enormous free breakfast. Then we were taken out to duck boats that were decked out in camouflage, complete with a stove, padded seats, and trained labrador retrievers. Two guys to a boat, along with two guides, and all the ammo we wanted. We went hunting there eight weeks in a row on the Sundays following our games, whether home or away.

The Wapello farmers would not hear of taking a red cent for this treatment. So we asked what we could do for them. They wondered if we could get them tickets to our last home game against Notre Dame. Well, all the tickets had been sold out weeks before. (This was the team that won the Rose Bowl and the National Championship that year.) So Bill Lapham, our center, went to see Evashevski to see if we could get 12 tickets for the guides. Evy did better than that. There were no regular seats left, so he got them sideline passes. The day of the game it was raining and blowing—perfect duck hunting weather. The guides showed up dressed in their waders and hunting gear, complete with their duck calls. Evy had a special bench for them right behind the team. Those guys proceeded to harangue the Notre Dame players and fans with duck calls and colorful language. We won by 14 points.

We hunted there for the next two seasons, and the guides always attended the last home game in their fancy attire and with the duck calls blowing LOUDLY.

Better Be Quick

After graduating from Iowa, I married an Iowa beauty, and we moved to my home state of California, where I spent the next 32 years teaching and coaching at the high school level. Much of what I used to motivate and encourage my students and athletes I took from what I learned under Coach Evashevski. Evy was a coach who could not abide mental mistakes. He was a very effective offensive coach. He was the first in the country, along with Dave Nelson of Delaware, to run the winged "T" offense. It took the Big Ten by storm.

When I came to Iowa as a 17-year-old freshman, there were 17 tackles on the freshman squad. I was far from being the best of the bunch. Probably not in the top ten. But I never missed even one practice, and once on the varsity as a sophomore, I tried not to make any mistakes. Evy liked players that did not make mistakes. I could not count the hours of time we would line up four teams in a square and take turns "getting off" on the quarterback cadence. Evy firmly believed that the offense had the advantage by knowing the "get off" call.

On the first day of practice in my sophomore year, Coach Evashevski gathered the team together in a set of bleachers and drove home that point in a very effective way. He called on one of the first-team players to come out and handed him a quarter. Instructing the player to hold out his hand, Evy placed the quarter in the player's palm. He told him to hold his hand out straight, and said he (Evy) was going to hold his own hand twelve inches above the young man's hand with his own hand palm up. He said he was going to turn his hand over and come down and pluck the coin before the player could close his hand. Evy explained that the first time the player saw the slightest movement, he was to close his hand.

Picture this: Ninety football players sitting in the bleachers watching the "Old Man" hold his hand a foot above that of the younger man and explaining how he was going to get that quarter. Evy's hand turned over and flashed down. The player, as quick as a cat, closed his hand. The two of them stood there, saying and doing nothing for what seemed like a long time. The young man opened his hand—surprise, no quarter. You know where the quarter was. That was a very effective way of showing the advantage that the offense has when it executes properly.

President Truman

When I left the Houston Oilers' training camp in July of 1961, it was too late in the year to get a job. Fortunately, Bob Hoff, my master teacher from the University of Iowa, had just taken a job as head football coach at Central Missouri State College in Warrensburg, Missouri. He heard of my availability and asked if I would come down and be his assistant coach and get my master's degree. So off we go!! Unfortunately, Hoff's job was to last only that one year.

Bob Hoff was a real go-go type. He wanted to do things his way. He often did not play by the rules, and this time it cost him his job. CMSC was at the bottom of the football ladder. They were bad, and the equipment we had was dangerous. We had leather helmets and most of the pants and jerseys were rotten, they were so old. Hoff had tried to get new gear, but to no avail.

We had a big Homecoming game coming up with our biggest rival, North West Missouri State at Marysville. Hoff was determined to beat them, and he figured out that one way to get the kids and fans fired up was to come out wearing new uniforms. He and I went to Kansas City to the Spaulding dealer, and he ordered $35,000 worth of gear without any authorization (bad move).

We were approaching Independence, Missouri on our way back from Kansas City, after the fatal purchase of the new football gear, and Bob said, "Let's stop and see if we can get President Truman to be the Grand Marshal at our Homecoming game." Why not? We pulled into the parking lot at the Truman Library and went inside. It was not very busy. We told the guard that we would like to speak with the President. He told us to stay there, and he was gone maybe two minutes. He came back and said, "Follow me." He took us to a fairly-large room and told us to have a seat. There was a couch, two tables, and four or five stuffed chairs in the room.

We sat down and looked around and wondered what was going on. A door opened at the far end of the room and in walked President Truman, dressed immaculately in a gray suit. He was not a very big man, and as he approached us we started to stand up. He raised his right hand and said, "Don't get up," as he quickly got to us and shook our hands while we were sitting down. He made us feel quite at ease.

I can't remember much of the conversation. I do remember telling him that when I was in the third grade in elementary school in Waseca, Minnesota, they let school out so we could go down to the train station and see him and listen to one of his famous whistle-stop speeches. He seemed to enjoy hearing that.

The one thing that stands out in my memory of that meeting was when Hoff began to tell the President of all the problems he was having as football coach at CMSC. Bob was about to ask him if he would be the Grand Marshal of the Homecoming Parade.

President Truman raised his hand and stopped Hoff in mid-sentence. He said, and I remember the exact words he spoke, "Young man, what kind of problems do you think I faced in making the decision to drop the Atomic Bomb?" Hoff stuttered around a few seconds, and then Mr. Truman changed the subject.

"Truman Speaks" presented to Charlie by President Truman in 1961.

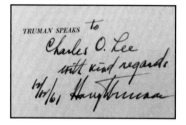

Personal autograph to Charlie by the President.

We had to have been with the President for at least 45 minutes when his aide came in and said something to him that we could not hear. President Truman excused himself and was gone maybe two minutes. When he returned, he said he was sorry but his wife had just called, and she was having trouble getting someone to clean off the driveway so he had to go take care of the matter (true story). When we got out in the hallway, the aide said that Mr. Truman wanted us to be shown around the library. This private tour took maybe an hour and was very entertaining. As we were about to leave, this same aide came up to us and handed each of us a book. It was the book entitled *Truman Speaks* and each copy was autographed to us by the President himself. Needless to say, that book is one of my most treasured possessions to this day.

Now I ask you—-Could something like that happen today? NO WAY!

Final Note on Bob Hoff

In an effort to get the kids fired up for the Homecoming game, Hoff hanged himself in effigy. We (I say we, because he had all the grad assistants help) hanged him from the flag pole in the middle of the quad. We used a wrestling takedown dummy that I had to hide in our bedroom until the event happened.

We still lost-

—C

Bob Hoff was released by Central Missouri State College in December of 1961 after a controversy over the unauthorized purchase of football equipment.

Iowa mascot Herky on display in Iowa Athletic Hall of Fame. Shown with roses to celebrate the 50-year Rose Bowl reunion of the 1959 Rose Bowl Team.

Hawkeye Football!!

Emailed to friends by Ralphene in October of 2006 while Ralphene and Charlie were in Iowa City for the 50th reunion celebration of the 1957 and 1959 Rose Bowl Teams.

Okay football fans—here's how we do it in Hawkeye Land!! We arrived in Iowa City Thursday evening. The team is staying at the Riverside Casino, a brand new hotel/casino. We got here and met our good friends Ruth and Dick Clausen. Friday started with a lunch for the team at the lovely Hall of Fame Building. The wives went to a luncheon at a nearby country club. I did not want to be far away, so I hung around the Hall of Fame. I went to the second floor where the awesome exhibits are. I could also look over the railing and see what was going on and hear every word once the speeches started. Sure beats a ladies' luncheon in my book!

Anyway, this was a reunion of the 25-year Rose Bowl team of Hayden Fry, and the 50-year reunion for the 1957 and 1959 teams. I can see why Charlie wanted so badly to attend. Everyone came up to him to talk. Everyone had a Charlie story! And he told a lot of stories himself. (His speech might have been hard to understand, but that didn't matter among these old friends!) Evy and Ruth were there. Evy is 89, they said. Hayden Fry there too, of course. The Hawk Booster club officers spoke; Jim Zabel emceed it all. They introduced each guy on each of the three teams and all the coaches. You talk about Memory Lane!

Charlie played four years of varsity ball. During those four years Iowa won three Big Ten titles, two Rose Bowl Championships, and one National Title! Not bad, huh? No wonder they still call that era the "Glory Days" and still say the '58 team is the best of all time. (Beat Cal 38-12 in the Rose Bowl!) After the lunch, there was an autograph session. Men, women, and kids lined up clear around the Hall of Fame Building, waiting to get in to get autographs. Only in Iowa!! It was great to see these guys signing footballs, hats, helmets, etc. for adoring fans.

After that, the guys went to watch the current team practice. Then the wives joined them for a tour of the new Kinnick Press Box. What a place! This was followed by a reception at the Hayden Fry Football Complex. I had a chance to talk to both Mr. and Mrs. Evy. Ruth commented on our yearly Christmas cards, and remembered that we were on our way east to Maryland. What incredible people those two are! (I did not remember that Evy retired at age 42. Jim Zabel's words were—"If this guy had not retired at 42, no one would even remember the name Bear Bryant!!")

After this, we boarded the huge Iowa Hawkeye buses that transported us to most of the functions, and were off to attend the pep rally held in the Pentacrest. Nanc, Sone— we attended a few of those Homecoming rallies in our day, but man, have they changed! Huge stage, lights, music, glitz, etc. and a sea of fans stretched as far as the eye could see. Each team was introduced, and then each guy stepped to the mic and said their name, position, and year. Many said "Go Hawks," and stuff like that. When it was Charlie's turn at the mic, he said his name, etc. as clear as a bell, and added, "Take No Prisoners!" The crowd LOVED that! After the pep rally, buses brought us back to the hotel. We left at 10:30 this morning for the day's festivities and got home about 9 pm. We leave at 7:30 am tomorrow for the tailgating party. The stadium parking lot was filled with motor homes tonight when the buses left. Game starts at 11 am. We did not sign up for the banquet tomorrow night, but now Charles wants to go, so I made arrangements, and we will. I am worn out. He is going strong and loving it! His speech gets harder to understand as the day goes on, but we work around that. Each person received a t-shirt and Hawkeye reunion hat at the reception. Wives, too. Guys will be introduced tomorrow at halftime. Evy, Hayden Fry, etc. are chauffeured everyplace in a stretch limo. They are doing this whole thing right. Now all we gotta do is Win the Darn Game tomorrow!! For those of you who are football fans, I hope you appreciate this. It has just been a wonderful event, and has meant so much to Charlie! Watch the game tomorrow, and Go Hawks!

Love, Ralphene and Charlie

P.S. The Hawkeyes defeated Purdue by a score of 47-17!

Mark Manders, Charlie, and Al Dunn at the tailgating party at the 2006 reunion of the 1957 and 1959 Rose Bowl teams held in Iowa City, Iowa.

Charlie autographing helmets for Iowa fans who were attending the 2006 Homecoming game versus Purdue.

The Hawkeye locker room on November 7, 1959 after defeating Minnesota by a score of 33-0. "Floyd of Rosedale" was at stake!

Charles and Ralphene Lee's wedding party, December 10, 1960. L-R: Nancy Elliott née Noll, Harriet Lenarz née Bryant, Sharon Moxley née Cantwell, Sonja Hofmeister née Boshart, Ralphene Lee née Ward, Dr. Earnest Matthews, Rev. Gilbert Stout, Charles Lee, Dick Clark, Bob Moerke, Bruce Lee, Al Dunn.

This photo of Charlie and Ralphene captioned "Football Pays for This Honeymoon" reappeared in the December 2014 edition of the Des Moines Register *as the "Old Time Photo of the Week."*

CAUTION FISH STORIES AHEAD

A♥ K♥ Q♥ J♥ 10♥

INTERESTS

Charlies RogueFort Dressing
1. Grate ½ lbs Finest "R" cheese - Fine
2. Add juice ½ lemon
3. Dash Tabasco
4. 1 cup Sour Cream
5. 1 cup Mayonnaise

Gramps printed this ☺

Interests

By Ralphene

Athletics played a major part in Charlie's life. His passion for football and wrestling are common knowledge and are documented in this book, but he was also an exceptional baseball player from his early years, playing American Legion baseball, high school ball, and through his freshman year in college. (He was offered a $3,000 bonus to sign with the Pittsburg Pirates right out of high school, but turned it down to play football at Iowa.) He might have continued his collegiate baseball career but for the intervention of Coach Forest Evashevski, who really gave him no choice!

Charlie was introduced to the joys of the outdoor life at a very early age. His father was very influential, as was his grandfather, William Young. Charlie and Bruce spent many hours together hunting and fishing. While Bruce's first love was hunting, Charlie's was fishing, although each enjoyed both to the utmost. Most of all, they enjoyed spending time together.

Charlie loved virtually every kind of fishing, from the farm ponds of Iowa and the Skunk River, to the trout steams of California, Montana, Idaho, and British Columbia. His years as a fishing guide with his good friend Bill Hickey produced some of his fondest memories. Tight lines!

In addition to his love of athletics and the out-of-doors, Charlie filled his life with other interests, not the least of which was playing cards: any kind of poker, cribbage, spades, hearts, bridge, pinochle, canasta, Old Maid, Go Fish, you name it, he played it…and won!

I don't know where Charlie got the gambling gene, certainly not from his parents, Florence and Big Charlie. He loved to play poker and quickly became very good at it.

One reason I did not object to this pastime is that I knew what kind of card player he really was. His friends would often say, "That Charlie Lee is the luckiest guy I know!" But what they did not realize, was that he was a true student of the game. He had an extensive library of books written by the pros and was always on the lookout for more. He studied the big players at the big games, and learned a lot that way. He was a master at recognizing "tells" and certainly had the perfect "poker face" when he was at the tables. He knew the odds, and he had the patience to wait until they were in his favor.

Charlie did not record many of his adventures at the gambling tables. I wish he had, because he had some interesting stories, for sure! In a 2005 email to Targe Lindsay he states, "You wouldn't believe some of the things I have experienced. Once I was at a poker table at the time a guy in the game was shot and killed. Another time, shotgun-toting robbers held up the game at the Camino Casino."

He would bet on almost anything, and one of his favorite phrases was, "I"ll flip you for it!" His friends quickly learned to shy away from that one! Each guest at his memorial service received a red, white, and black poker chip with his picture on each side—the picture of him in his Iowa football days on one side, the other side a picture of him as a Bella Vista coach.

Charlie liked to cook and was eager to try any recipe that sounded good to him. His meals were always delicious, so you might say that he was a gourmet. He also loved to eat, and would go to any type of restaurant, from a half-smoke stand on the streets of D.C. to a Five Star restaurant, usually ordering the most exotic offering on the menu, regardless of price, so you might say he was a gourmand.

He was an avid and knowledgeable chess player, playing online with people all over the world. He sponsored and coached the Bella Vista chess club for a few years, arranging competitions and taking the kids to these events.

Charlie was an always-available mentor, an avid gardener, dependable friend, an artist when it came to fly tying, an always-tough competitor, and a seldom-but-good loser, who was committed to living a life of excellence to its fullest.

Interests

Charlie with a group of his fishing buddies in Kalispell, Montana in 1989.

Charlie and Susie fishing together on one of many family camping trips.

Charlie, Sam, and Bruce with Bruce's drift boat at the Power House in Ennis, Montana, 1997.

A Friend's Perspective
By Targe Lindsay

It was clear to me that Charlie was a special kind of guy over thirty years ago, but it was during his last few years, when he and I played a lot of chess in the Lee home, that I really got to know him and of his many skills, interests, ventures, and of the ongoing devotion that his former wrestlers and PE students held for him. Most of you saw that on display at his memorial service.

I tried to sum up what I knew of him while getting prepped to MC that evening. I cannot remember how much of it I mentioned then, but since he was in the news re the Sac-Joaquin Section Hall of Fame, and since there was no way the Bee writer could have known or had the space to do him justice, here it is in full, as best I can put it.

As we all know, Charlie was a unique person: multi-faceted, multi-talented, and multi-motivated. Although he was not rich and famous, he was interesting to all who knew him, and perhaps it was he, not the guy with the beard in the beer commercial, who was the most interesting man in the world. Consider:

He was loyal and committed to each identity he assumed—from a Tom Sawyeresque kid to San Juan Spartan, Iowa Hawkeye, BV Bronco, and Godfather Emeritus to many who met him along the way.

He was a gifted athlete and most likely the only Big Ten football player ever to play five full years on Big Ten, Rose Bowl, and National Championship teams…after competing with one hundred five other freshmen for the scholarships offered by Iowa.

He had the gifts of insight and judgment. He was playing winning poker and knew when to hold 'em and knew when to fold 'em before Kenny Rogers ever cut the record. While a student at Iowa University, and visiting Ralphene's parents, he won a Chrysler Imperial from a farmer who was a veteran player at the VFW's Friday night poker game, much to the chagrin of Ralphene's parents. A couple years earlier his poker playing got him evicted from the university dorm. Win some, lose some.

He had a sense of what is important in life early on when he gave up a shot at the NFL's Houston Oilers in order to settle down with

Ralphene and raise a family in one home, in one place. He was intuitive, practical, and determined…A magnet who drew serious-minded kids, and their parents who wanted the best for their kids, to his wrestling program. Both a strategical and tactical thinker, as well as a practitioner who knew how to get the best out of each kid and how to use them all together to win some 245 dual meets and numerous tournaments…resulting in district, section, state, national, and Olympic champions…also resulting in recognition for his program and Hall of Fame recognition for David, Charlie, and Ralphene.

A teacher for thousands of kids and mentor for many, including Dave Schultz, who was assistant wrestling coach at Stanford when David wrestled there. Dave, an Olympic Champion, called Charlie for help with his game plan before some of his biggest personal Olympic and world-level matches.

A low-key charmer, no doubt, for I recall that all of the women teachers at BV liked Charlie. A Pied Piper whom teenage boys would follow anywhere.

A super salesman who could easily sell 98-pound teenage boys on not eating, or running several miles in order to lose weight.

An intimidator whose teams won a few points before they even wrestled when they marched out into the gym in all-white warm-ups.

An entrepreneur and organizer who funded his wrestling program by holding a popular tournament at the end of each wrestling season, and who teamed up with one of his most capable adversaries to form a guide service for fishermen.

A colleague who could elicit the help of many to pull off such events.

A practical joker, and sometimes relentless teaser, always without malice.

A competitor who went for the jugular with a smile on his face.

A compassionate coach who treated all his wresters alike, win or lose.

A true believer in a work ethic. When asked what a wrestler had to do to be good, he said, "Never miss practice."

An intrepid traveler, much on the go, but never in the air.

A fisherman's fisherman who could find the fish wherever they were lurking, if any were.

A professional who shared camaraderie and close quarters in an office with four other coaches, a ruthlessly honest but adult group, for over twenty years...all men who told it like it was, win or lose, giving feedback concerning the teams and the kids they coached.

The Gold Standard for the many other BV and area coaches he coached with and against through the years.

A confidant for many and a spur for many others.

A chef who was proud of his cooking and who the home economics teachers invited in to cook chili for their classes every December...with a secret ingredient that he smuggled on campus to their delight and...to the chagrin of his teetotaler principal.

A gourmet cook and a gourmand himself as he and Ralphene explored and probably ate at almost every restaurant in Sacto County and others far and wide. A man with savory priorities who never looked at the price.

A chess player with worldwide experience over many years, thanks to the internet.

A lover and owner of several boats, the last one in which he got skunked, but he enjoyed each outing nevertheless.

A quiet man. How many of you ever heard him raise his voice? A forceful, but wily man, one who almost always got his way.

A plain-spoken man who gave you the unvarnished truth, comfortable or not. A writer of memories and letters of recommendation for many wrestlers.

A brave man. Unbeknownst to Ralphene beforehand, at a gathering of BV athletes, he once invited all the wrestlers who had wrestled for him to come to their place for a spaghetti dinner two days later. One hundred showed up...and one hundred ate spaghetti.

A family man and near-perfect grandfather whom every family member revered. His three grandchildren became his pride and joy and a major interest in his life, as he was in theirs, as he taught them character-building precepts by example, play, and practice.

A dog's best friend.

A rational man who knew when to give up driving and boating, but never coaching, which he did in his living room when the current BV coach, Mike Lee, and his wrestlers came to hear what he had to say or point out on video or on the living room floor.

A patient man who countered Mr. Parkinson with skill and perseverance for twenty-plus years, and although he lost mobility and the power of articulate speech, he maintained an agile brain and dexterity in his hands...as proven by the hundreds of exquisite fly fishing flies he tied in later years. No one ever heard him complain through those years, nor did he complain after going fishing thirty-two times on the Sacramento River without a strike when the salmon did not show up two years ago.

An unembarrassed, but appreciative recipient of physical support from his brother, Bruce. Like two peas in a pod, he and Bruce resonated with practical assumptions and unspoken brotherly love. Riding shotgun all the way, Bruce has been indispensable to the health and emotional welfare of both Charlie and Ralphene.

In Charlie's later rounds with Parkinson's, although he sometimes lost equilibrium, he never lost his poise, and at the end of the struggle he endured some takedowns, but eventually escaped with style points.

Several hundred people came to honor him that night, filling up almost all of the bleachers on one side of the gym. Rightly so.

—Targe

Without Targe Lindsay this book never would have come about. It was his suggestion that got Charlie started writing, and his encouragement that kept him going. Targe has also been my sounding board and editor throughout the whole process. I can hardly find words to express my thanks. —Ralphene

Fourteen Days

It was July of 1968, and the family was back in Mt. Pleasant for the summer. We always enjoyed "Poverty Knob," as Ralphene's dad, Ralph, liked to refer to the 22 acres just inside the city limits. There was a small house and a couple of barns where he kept the horses that Ralphene rode, and a wonderful garden that Nina tended. It was just a fun place to spend summer vacation, particularly for the kids. Both kids showed horses in shows all around the state. They had a blast, and their mother usually took home the gold.

I spent most days at Oakland Mills fishing for catfish, or at the local farm ponds catching bass. One day after reading an article in *Sports Afield Magazine* entitled, "Little Known Streams of the West" by Joe Brooks (a well-known outdoor writer) I thought it sounded like it would be fun to fish those streams. So, with my wife's blessing, on July 14th, 1968 I started out. What follows is an account of that trip, taken from a log that I kept of the whole experience.

7/14/68 Started from Mt. Pleasant, Iowa in our Volkswagen camper with 8,267 miles on the odometer. Filled up in Council Bluffs, Iowa, 13.2 gallons, $3.80. Traveled to Lexington, 8,528 mileage, 19 gallons of gas, $5.15. Had a blowout right rear tire at 8,633 miles, 20 miles west of Lincoln, Nebraska, mile 8,795.

7/15 10.4 gallons of gas, $3.10 at Scotts Bluff, Nebraska. Also bought some pop and ice $1.46. Mileage 9,039. $3.40 for 11 gallons gas at Casper, Wyoming.

7/16 Bought Wyoming fishing license and supplies at Lander, Wyoming, $8.75. Fished the Popo Agi River just east of Lander and caught 6 trout from 14 inches to 20 inches, 3 brown and 3 rainbow. Lost 5 more good-sized fish. This is a small stream, and I asked the rancher's permission to fish (no problem). I would rate the fishing 8 on a scale of 10. 9,495 miles, $4.55 gas, $2.65 food. Camped 25 miles out of Lander in Sinks Canyon. Fished small lake in the morning, but no luck.

7/17 Went back to the Popo Agi, caught 4 fish 13 1/2 inches to 15 inches, all browns. Camped at Buck's Lake, caught probably 40 fish from 6-10 inches, all on the humpy.

7/18 Afternoon of the 18th, camped at the edge of the Teton Wilderness. I walked about 1 1/2 miles up Pacific Creek, only two small trout for my trouble. Caught 15 large whitefish. I am pooped.

7/19 Fished the Hobart River south of Jackson Hole. It is big water, compared to what I have been fishing. I caught 16 big, fat, healthy cutthroat trout. Good campground. Camped on the Green River just out of Pinedale, Wyoming. Beautiful water, also big water. Fished only a short while. Very windy. Caught two small 8-inch rainbows. Asked around town about fishing. An old well-weathered local sent me to a small stream 27 miles out of Daniel, Wyoming. A stream named Horse Creek. What a find. After checking in at the forest ranger station, I headed up a dusty road that had not seen a tire track in quite a while. I was all alone. Saw many ducks and geese, four giant beavers, and two elk. Fished Horse Creek for one hour. Caught three brook trout, 12 to 14 inches, 15 cutthroat, all about 14 inches. The fly fishing is just fantastic. You can wade the entire stream. I don't think there is a soul within 10 miles. Will fish again in the morning.

7/20 Am camped on the Salt River near Afton, Wyoming. Will fish in the morning. Came here from Big Pine, 60 miles, on not-too-good dirt road. Saw lots of game and some truly-beautiful country. The Salt River looks like a dream come true for the dry fly fisherman. I must say, I thought I knew most of the large rivers in the West that had good trout fishing, but I had never heard of the Salt River. It is about 30 yards wide with a hard bottom, averages three to four feet deep with smooth-running water. I started fishing at 7:30 pm. I caught one rainbow, 14 inches. At 8 pm a hatch came on that you would have to see to believe. Some real hogs started to surface feed. I didn't know which fish to cast for first. I really got FISH FEVER. Try as I might, I could not even get a rise to my offerings. I literally tried every fly in my boxes. NOTHING. Am going to the nearest tackle shop and will try again in the morning.

7/21 No luck.

7/22 Drove to Logan, Utah and spent a day or two with Pat and Roy Erickson. Pat really knows her way around a stove (great meals, after my own cooking). Roy beat me at golf—guess it's time to go.

7/23 Drove to Dillon, Montana to fish the Big Hole, but got waylaid in Dell, a sleepy burg of 22 people. Store, gas station, and bar, all in one building. The proprietor told me about Sheep Creek. (Brooks had mentioned it in his article.) It was high up in the Gravely Range Mountains. A beautiful little stream that ran about 1/2 mile through a small meadow before plunging down the mountain to enter the Red Rock River. Saw two other fishermen with spin poles. They had had no luck. I fished for about three hours, caught five brook trout, 13-15 inches, and lost many more. Will try again in the morning. Used a grey humpy.

7/24 Fished four hours, caught lots of fish, kept four 13-17 inchers. The 17-incher was a real good fish for that water. Gave the four trout to the gal at the store-bar-office-gas station complex. Fished the Red Rock River by Dell. The locals say there are lots of big (4-6 pound) fish in the Rock. I had no luck at all. Too much brush and blowdowns for my liking. Arrived Ennis, Montana at 6 pm. Bought some flies and leaders. Saw Old Tom. Fished for two hours just below Cameron. Man, this is THE river. Caught five rainbows, 1 1/2-2 pounds. Lost two fish probably 3-4 pounds, maybe more. They got in the current and that's all. River is in perfect shape. For big trout the Madison is the river. Will try again in the morning.

7/25 Fished hard all day 8:30 to 5 pm. Caught lots of fish, 13-15 inches, caught two rainbows 17 and 18 inches respectively. I lost others and had three strikes from some huge fish. I had to work hard for what I got. The thing that is so neat about this river is that you know that if you put in a hard day's fishing, you will have a chance to catch a trophy fish.

3,800 miles later, in summing up the trip, I thoroughly enjoyed the two weeks of fishing by myself. There is something about being able to do just as you please, go where you want without having to depend on someone else, that is most satisfying. However, two weeks for me was just about right. I found that after that amount of time I became lonesome for home and hearth. The trip provided me a chance to see a great deal of new country and retrace some old footsteps. (Old Tom was a retired rancher about 85 years old who

Barry Rannells and I had played poker with in the Silver Dollar Saloon a few years earlier.)

Each stream I fished seemed to offer something new as far as type of water, kind and size of fish, type of terrain, and degree of fishing success. If I had to pick one stream and one day on the trip where I enjoyed my greatest success and had the most fun, I would pick my first day of fishing on the Popo Agi River just outside Lander, Wyoming. I had not expected to catch anywhere near the number or size of trout that I caught that day. Any dry pattern worked, I did not see another angler, and the weather and stream conditions were perfect. If I had to pick my favorite fishing spot, it would be a hard choice, for there were many excellent ones. I would pick the Madison River just outside of Ennis along the Cameron Flats. There is something about that river that fascinates me. The terrain is not as pretty as some of the places I fished. Sometimes the wind blows so hard you can only handle ten feet of line. And some periods, for days on end, the fishing is terribly slow. But even on a dead fishing day, a good fisherman who works hard (stays in the water six or seven hours straight) will catch some fish and he will always get a few strikes from some really big fish. And therein lies the secret. It is those big fish—they are there, and you know that at some point you are going to hook one. If you happen to be lucky and hit a good day, you will get some of the best trout fishing anywhere.

I was gone a total of 14 days, traveled 3,800 miles, spent a total of $124 for EVERYTHING. Wish I could go again!

In 2004, David recreated parts of his dad's trip—fishing many of his favorite streams—also by himself.

The Charliebill Fishing and Guide Service—first guide service on the American River.

Fishing Guide

I always loved to fish—particularly for trout, steelhead, and salmon. So when I had a chance to do it, and maybe make a little money on the side, I went for it.

I met Bill Hickey the year I started teaching and coaching at Bella Vista. He was the wrestling coach at El Dorado High School in Placerville. That was in 1962. We shared a lot of things in common—one being a love of fishing. In 1975 we took a steelhead fishing trip to the Klamath River in Northern California. We stayed at Al Kutzkey's lodge right on the river. That was our first introduction to drift boat fishing. It was love at first bite! Our guide was a young fellow just starting out. Al was giving him a second chance. The kid had been heavy into the drug scene and was really messed up. But the guide business turned him around, and he straightened out. He became one of the top steelhead guides in the West. On our trip with him we had a great time, caught lots of fish, and made plans for a return trip. After a couple more fishing trips, we thought that there were a few things that our guides did that we could do even better (getting rigged up ahead of time, having the proper gear, and above all, providing a great on-the-river lunch). Our wives were supportive, so we made plans to start the Charliebill Fishing Guide Service. Bill gets all the credit for the name. We purchased a new 17-foot Alumaweld drift boat (guide series). I think it cost us $1,800.

Interests

You have to know Bill Hickey to appreciate this, but he is Mr. Organization to the hilt and beyond. We bought out our local wholesale fishing dealer. We had plenty of tackle, plus hats and t-shirts that advertised "Charliebill Chili Tastes Better on the River," and we became famous for our "Charliebill Early Morning Toddy"—a mixture of hot chocolate and rum. We charged $90 for two people. For that price, they received a full eight hours on the river. Any fish caught, we cleaned and packaged. Lunch consisted of New York strip steak, baked potato, salad, rolls with butter, wine, and homemade apple or cherry pie for dessert. We always had snacks available—Cokes, coffee, nuts, chips, apples or some other kind of fruit. For a while this really went over big. It was a huge commitment on our part, getting all this ready. The guys who brought their wives or girlfriends along thought it was just fantastic. We had two custom-made grills that fit perfectly in the boat.

On one trip to the Klamath River, we were followed downriver by a local guide and his two clients, a man and his wife. We were all catching fish, so we stayed pretty much together, just shooting the bull and saying how great life was. At noon we all pulled into shore for lunch. The other guide built a fire (it was a cold day) and while his clients warmed themselves, he broke out a can of beans and cut two sticks to grill hot dogs. Bill set up four folding chairs and our portable table and grill, and proceeded to grill thick New York steaks. He passed around a bottle of GOOD wine, but it was too cold for that, so he gave each person a steaming cup of Charliebill Toddy. While the steaks were cooking, we brought the two boat heaters up and set them in place to provide a comfortable setting. This was almost too much for the other guide. He had never seen such service. His clients didn't say anything, but you could see they were impressed. That night Bill got a phone call from the husband wanting to book a trip. (Pays to advertise.)

As time went on, however, and we began to get a more serious type of fisherman, the lunch went by the boards. The real steelheader did not want to spend 1 1/2 or 2 hours eating lunch. We could understand that. We were the first guides on the American River, and I believe the first ones to run a drift boat in the entire area. To be a fishing guide in California at that time, all you needed to do was to pay a $30 license fee and post a $1,000 bond. But there are guides, and then again, there are GUIDES. Bill and I already knew quite a bit about steelhead and salmon fishing, and we were quick learners. There are some things that you would think would be common sense. Things like being on time, having top-flight gear, and making sure it was in top condition. Having things arranged so if a customer lost a rigging, another was in his hands immediately. Always try and stay one step ahead of the customer's needs.

The thing about being a steelhead and salmon guide is that sooner or later you are going to have to learn to run whitewater. There is always that first time. When we got the drift boat, we spent hours on the American River learning how to row. It is not at all like rowing a normal boat. You most always *head into* trouble (big waves, rocks, turbulence, etc.) and *pull away* from it. Bill and I got so we could hold a boat in place in the middle of a rapids. Eventually we were pretty fair artists. We fished the American, the Feather, and the Yuba. (A client of Bill's caught a 17-lb. steelhead on the Yuba just after lunch on a wiggle wart.) We fished the Klamath, the Rogue, and the Deschutes in Western Oregon. I also took the drift boat on my yearly summer trips to Montana. We fished the Madison (mostly), the Big Hole, the Yellowstone, and the Henry's Fork. Some great memories there. Those waters are not very challenging from a rowing standpoint, but you can never relax on the water. My good friend, Barry Alan, turned my brother's drift boat over twice in one day on the Madison.

In the eight years I was in the guide business, we only had two close calls. We (Bill and I) were running gear boats on the Klamath River for this guide—I can't remember his name right now. He and another guide each had two clients. We would leave ahead of them, get to a prearranged spot and set up lunch. After the clients had eaten, we would clean up and head downriver and set up camp for the night and prepare dinner. Since this was our first time on this section of the Klamath, the one guide would go over the map of the river for the next day, pointing out which side of the river to run, where to go and not to go. By now we had had enough experience to be able to stand up in the boat and read most water ahead. This particular day we were running a tough section of the river. There was one spot that was fairly tricky if you took the wrong line. As it turned out, this guy gave us bad information. From a rowing position it looked for all the world that you would run the left side, but that was wrong, you needed to go right. That way was a piece of cake. By the time we realized we were wrong, it was too late. We were swept up against a huge boulder and in the blink of an eye, the boat was full of water. That was fortunate, because it made us real heavy and instead of being swept into a bad rapids, we made it to an eddy where we bailed out the boat and moved on. All our gear was tied down, and everything was stored in waterproof bags, so we were lucky. We just got a good scare and a dunking. That night we had an interesting discussion with the guide!

The other close call was my fault. It came real close to being a BAD situation. We were again on the Klamath. This time it was a pleasure trip with Bill and me, Bill's son, and his friend. We were approaching a run known as Little Blossom, an unrunnable stretch of water. You would pull over to the right bank and line your boat down. You needed to approach LB on the left side of the river, and then pull real hard to the right side. The current was pretty fast, so you needed to start your pull early and really lay into the oars. Bill's son, Mike, was ahead of us and he made it just fine. I started my pull, but miscalculated a little. I was nearly in the safe eddy, but not quite. I was about a yard short, but that was almost deadly. I was pulling like crazy, but was just about to be swept over the rim of Little Blossom, when the front end of the boat touched a small rock that was sticking out of the water about six inches. It stopped our progress for about two seconds, but that was just enough for Mike to grab the gunnel and pull us into the eddy. Just lucky!!

We had a lot of fun trips. We didn't make any real money, but it was a good tax write-off. One of our fishing offerings was a five-day, four-night trip on the Deschutes River in Northwest Oregon. It was quite an undertaking, but Bill was up to the challenge. We hired a local guide in Madras, Oregon. I would drive up with the drift boat, meet the guide, talk with him about the trip, meet the clients at the motel we had reserved for them, and the next morning we would hit the river. The Deschutes had some very challenging whitewater. I had fished it once before with Bill and a couple of friends on a trip where we were the customers. Bill had fished it once before that. He had told me about the water and had even taken some video of the trip. He had put a rather nasty dent in the front end of the boat, which happened on that trip. He hit a rock in White Horse Rapids, a really tough piece of water. You would not run into White Horse until the third day of the trip. Bill kept talking and talking about how bad it was. That there had been several boaters lose their lives on White Horse. So the day we were set to run it, I was PSYCHED!! The guide we were with started out ahead of us. Now I could hear this big roar of a rapids. I thought, "I hope I'm up to this" (my goodness). The guide pulled over to the right bank and motioned for us to follow. He said we always looked at this rapids before we would run it, just so he could show us the right line and how to set up the boat, in order to hopefully avoid any major mistakes. So we climbed up to the railroad tracks and walked about 1/4 mile where we could get a good look at the rapids. There it was. Two miles of exciting water. The first 300 yards were class 4 1/2 to class 5 rapids and the rest class 2 and 3.

Right at the top of the rapids was the infamous "Oh Shit Rock" and wrapped tightly around it was a drift boat. It was aptly named. The guide said the water was up a little, but that was good. OK. He then proceeded to tell me how we would run it. I had had quite a bit of experience running whitewater by now. But this was intimidating. After studying the water for about 15 minutes, we were off. If I thought the pre-rapids was loud, it was nothing compared to White Horse itself. The guide was about 100 yards ahead of us and then he seemed to just drop off the edge of the world. Here we go. Everything happened so fast. There's Oh Shit Rock, two hard pulls right, slide just off the left side, change directions, pull left, straighten up, pull hard across five yards to another run, spin boat 180° and pull like mad to a tight eddy and stop. That's it. Takes about 20 seconds. Then the next couple of miles seems like a piece of cake (but you better not lose your concentration)!

I fished the Deschutes four times. It was on the fourth trip that I had the most embarrassing moment of my life. Bill had arranged a trip for four guys from San Jose. I was to meet them in Madras, pick up the other guide, and enjoy five days of fishing. And this type of trip made us some $. Everything was going as planned; we met the clients for breakfast, and then it was off to the river. On the Deschutes you may not fish from the boat. All fishing is done from shore or wading. It was the second day out and the other guide and I had planned the day's agenda. He was to lead, and we would do our own thing for lunch and meet at a designated spot to camp and have dinner. Well, in the course of the day, I was fishing on one side of a rather large island and did not see him pass me by. And he didn't realize what had happened.

So when he reached our campsite and I was not there, he thought I missed it and went on downriver. When I got to the spot, I got the gear out of the boat and started to make camp. But after a while it dawned on me that he was not coming. That we must have passed each other somewhere along the line. I informed the clients, who were not too thrilled, and we loaded up the boat and headed downstream. It was getting dark and White Horse Rapids was not too far off. I had no intention of trying that in the dark. We pulled into shore and got out the sleeping bags. The other guide had the food and tents. The night was fairly chilly, and it rained on us. The two guys that were with me took it pretty well, considering they were paying $1,000 each for the privilege of sleeping in the rain with no supper and a guide who looked like he didn't know from sic-em.

We loaded up the boat at first light and headed downriver. It wasn't too long before we came upon the other boat. They had spent the night mostly sitting around a campfire to keep warm, having no sleeping bags. But at least they stayed dry in the tents. We fixed them a big breakfast. They were good sports about the whole thing. Said this would give them something to talk about. It was a trip I would not forget. After breakfast we set off downriver to run White Horse Rapids. We got out just below the pre-rapids and walked the railroad tracks for a look at White Horse. The clients were impressed and a little intimidated. Two of them decided to walk around the rapids. One rode with me, and the other went with the other guide. After the trip was over I sent the two who had run the rapids a special t-shirt with a picture of a horse that read, "I rode the White Horse." Not many people knew what that meant, but they did.

We were always looking for ways to promote the business. We took Gary Vogt (outdoor editor for the Bee) on a free trip, as well as the outdoor writer for the *San Francisco Examiner* and his wife and granddaughter. Got some very nice write-ups. But the thing that really put us on the map was when we were written up in *Sunset Magazine* and *Outdoor Life*. The phone was ringing off the hook. The good thing about our service was that a fisherman from the Bay Area, or any place in between, could drive to Sacramento, fish the American River with us, and drive back home that same day. Other than that, they would have to go to the Klamath, and you were looking at three days minimum.

The only problem was, steelhead fishing took a turn for the worse after about three years. A strain of steelhead called Washougal, that had been developed in Washington state, died off. I think it had to do with some low water-flow. At any rate, good steelhead fishing was gone. There were many times I would fish two clients all day and not catch a fish. I hated that. Most of the clients were pretty good about it when they realized I was doing everything right, but there just were no fish. The thing that saved us was salmon season. That was always good, and we caught lots of fish.

It was now 1984, and David graduated from high school and was wrestling for Stanford. Many of his matches were on Saturday, and Ralphene and I did not want to miss any of his competition. So that was the end of my guiding adventure. Bill kept guiding and even bought a jet sled with which he had a lot of success. A little aside—right after he bought the sled, he was on the river learning how to run it. He made a quick turn and launched himself from the boat. Fortunately, he was wearing a kill switch so he just got wet. I would have liked to have seen that!

A couple years after Bill got his sled, I bought one also. It was a 17-foot Fish Rite with a 90-horse Yamaha jet. With some help from Bill, I got to be a pretty fair jetboat pilot. It is very different from a regular motor. The first time I ran the Feather River, I was going flat out, about 35 mph when I came to a sandbar, probably not more than two or three inches deep. My first instinct was to slow down. Bill was with me and shouted, "GIVE IT THE GAS, don't cut her back!" I did, and we just skipped over the bar tic, tic, tic. Scary as hell. I learned to run that boat and enjoyed several years of river-running with it. I sold it to a young guy for $10,000, a real bargain. The boat had been especially made for the Sacramento Boat Show. I bought it right off the floor. It had two-tone blue paint with scrolling, electric trolling motor, large gas tank, special bottom, etc. The young guy used to call me once a year and tell me how much fun he was having taking his son fishing. I haven't heard from him for a couple of years.

I recall one humorous incident, although I didn't think so at the time. On one of our five-day trips to the Deschutes River, I had to miss a couple days of school, so I took sick leave. Somehow or other, the writer for the Bee, Gary Vogt, was doing an article on steelhead fishing. He wrote a story about Bill and me and had a picture of me with my clients running whitewater. This article listed the dates and had quite a nice write-up about our trips. A member of the women's PE department, who was not a great fan of mine in those days, took the paper to Targe Lindsay, our principal, to show him how I was spending two of my "sick days." Targe could not ignore this, and I was docked two days' pay by the district. He always felt bad about that. That's how it goes.

Those eight years I spent as a river guide were truly enjoyable. I had more fishing trips on great water than I can even begin to list. I sure wish I could do it all over again!

Charlie and David with the original Charliebill drift boat, Ennis, Montana, summer of 1982.

Bill Hickey and Charlie on one of their many fishing trips together.

My Friend Bill

I first met Bill Hickey when he lived in Placerville and taught and coached wrestling at El Dorado High School. We enjoyed competing against each other and became good friends. We would have a dual meet against each other every year and then take the wives out for a big dinner. Bill's wife Marylou and Ralphene got along very well.

Since Bill and I loved to fish, we took many a memorable fishing trip together. We started the Charliebill Guide Service. Bill did all of the planning and organizing for the trips. If ever there was a man who could plan, it was Bill. Sometimes he would overdo. On one trip with my good friend Barry Rannells, Bill had everything planned out, down to how much time you had to spend behind the wheel. When your time was up THAT'S IT—stop and let the next guy drive. Drove Rannells crazy!

Bill was a very even-tempered guy. Hard to rile. However, I think sometimes our cribbage games would get to him. I recall one time on our way back from a fishing trip to the Campbell River, we were on the ferry and getting set to start our usual cribbage game. We had been playing for favors (not always money) and Bill owed me, as usual. So I said, "Bill, do me a favor and go down to the car and get the cribbage board." Since he owed the favor and this was not out of line, off he goes. It was a pretty long trip and when he gets back I say, "Where's the score pad?" He just looks at me, because he knows what's coming next. "Bill, do me a favor and go down and get the score pad." Barry Alan was along on the trip, and he never lets me forget about that one.

I can remember almost all of the fishing trips we took together, and there were a bunch. I went on literally hundreds of fishing trips with scores of different friends. But I always looked forward to going on ones that Bill and I went on together or which he was a part of. Montana (drunk as skunks at Pond's Lodge, playing pool and couldn't lose), Campbell River (Barry's boat bikini bait, best seafood dinner ever), Feather River (game warden lost my license, good news, bad news). In British Columbia, our guide runs into the rocks, and we both hit the deck—Bill had just had his hip replaced. Buying noodle rods, learning to bobber fish for steelhead, 12-foot rods, visits to Grants Pass and times on the Rogue. Eating so many shrimp I got hives. We used to say that a man makes many friends in a lifetime, but usually only has one partner (make that two, Marylou).

More Trips

I have been fortunate to have taken a lot of really fun trips, made even more so by my companions. I wanted to catch every species of freshwater fish in the U.S. I had caught all but the gar, muskie, and Atlantic salmon. (I know that salmon live most of their lives in the ocean, but I still consider them a freshwater fish.)

I made reservations to fish a beat on the Bonaventure River on the Gaspe Peninsula in New Brunswick. My brother Bruce and Barry Rannells went along. We took my GMC pickup which carried our Amerigo camper. This camper was really too big for my pickup, but Ralphene loved it. It was nice, but a bear to drive. We drove to Montana and spent a couple of days in Glacier National Park before crossing into Canada, just south of Cardston. It was while we were staying in the park that I caught my largest river trout ever, a 7-lb. 9-oz. beauty, caught in the Flathead River. From Cardston we headed for Medicine Hat where we picked up the Trans-Canada Hwy #1. We took that all the way (it changed #s a few times) to Gaspe, as far east as you could go. It was a rough ride every inch of the way. That Amerigo camper was miserable to drive—bump, bump, bump.

When we got to Quebec, I bought a fishing license and a few Atlantic salmon flies at $4 each. I also bought Barry a Royal Churchill cigar for $5—a BIG price. Barry saved it for over a year, until he smoked it on a trip to Montana. From Quebec until we reached the Gaspe, most everyone spoke French. There was one small town after another, each with its own sparkling-clean church. And a surprising number of the men wore suits. Each time we stopped for breakfast we were greeted by a big bowl of the best-tasting maple syrup you could imagine.

When we arrived at the town of Murdochville to fish the Bonaventure River, I was informed I was three days early and would just have to wait until my reservation date came up. We decided not to stick around. I tried to find some places to fish on my own, but had no luck. We headed home. One thing that we were looking forward to was a big lobster dinner in Bangor, Maine (the lobster capital of the world)! When we arrived in Bangor, there was not a lobster to be found in the whole town.

We drove to Boston, and it just so happened that the Red Sox were playing a game that day at Fenway Park. I have always been sorry we did not stop. We drove to New York where we dropped Barry off. Bruce and I traveled on to Mt. Pleasant, where we picked up Ralphene and the kids for the trip back to California. 6,500 miles.

Rolling Thunder
By Ralphene

Charlie was always an avid fly fisherman, and while we were in Maryland he researched several very famous streams for us to visit. One of his favorite spots was Mossy Creek, a lovely stream in Virginia, a little over an hour from our house. We had been there a couple times, and this particular trip was taking place in May. Actually, it was Thursday of Memorial Day weekend. I didn't think too much about that, and I later realized maybe I should have.

We started out early, and Charlie spent a couple hours on the stream and caught some pretty nice trout, which he released, as he usually did. We started home around 1 pm. Charlie was driving, and we pulled onto the highway that would take us north into

Washington, D.C. We drove for a few minutes, and I suddenly realized that there were crowds of people on all the overpasses waving American flags, holding signs, and cheering. Now I looked around and saw literally hundreds of motorcycles coming up behind us. Very soon they were surrounding us—and these were serious bikers! Charlie, meanwhile, had the window down, waving out the window, with the Star Spangled Banner blasting from his favorite CD. There were so many bikers—there was no way to get out of the group, and we were the only car or van I could spot in the whole caravan. Charlie was honking like crazy, and the bikers were all high-fiving him. He was having a ball!

I later learned that this was the annual event called the Rolling Thunder Run. It was first begun in 1988 by a group whose cause was to recognize the plight of the POWs and MIAs from the Vietnam War, and to call attention to the cause of leaving no men behind. It has grown to be a huge event in the D.C. area. To this day I am not sure whether Charlie carefully planned our trip home or if it was just coincidence. Knowing him…

Drink Up

Ralphene and I went to lunch the other day. It was a new restaurant that we had heard was quite good, and the prices were not too bad, considering the quality of the food. When the waitress asked if we would care for something to drink, Ralphene said, "Water is fine, thanks." I said, "I'll have a lemonade." During the meal I asked for a refill. The waitress took my glass and brought me another lemonade. Right away I knew what was coming. I had had an experience with a "new glass."

Barry Alan, Bill Hickey, and I had gone to Quadra Island in British Columbia to fish for salmon. We stayed at a beautiful little cabin right on the water. Barry had brought his boat, and we were having a great time. One day we caught a bunch of rock fish, and Bill cooked them in a deep-fat fryer he had brought along. We all agreed it was one of the best meals we had EVER eaten.

We were staying just across the inlet from a fancy lodge (April Point Lodge, if I recall) and restaurant. One day after a particularly good day of salmon fishing we were all tired and did not feel like cooking. I said, "Let's try the lodge—my treat." Barry and Bill thought that was a great idea. We showered, put on some clean clothes, hopped in the boat, and in five minutes we were sitting down to what turned out to be a memorable meal. After a full day on the water, you can become very dehydrated. Barry downed seven glasses of iced tea. No one thought much about it, because you got free refills of iced tea—right? WRONG! When I got the bill—$14 for iced tea. Bill had had a few whiskeys and was feeling no pain. He thought $14 for iced tea was hilarious and told the waitress to bring him a couple of iced teas. I nixed that order. Every time I'm at a restaurant and have a refill of iced tea, I think of that meal and those two good friends!

Bill Hickey, Charlie, and Barry Alan at April Point Lodge.

Ah, Youth

One of my ex-wrestlers, Tracy Yeates, has a son Luke, who is 11 years old, who Tracy said just loves to fish. Tracy is not much of a fisherman himself, and Luke had never been fishing until Tracy's friend Todd Gaston took Tracy and Luke bass fishing last year. Luke ended up catching three small bass, and Tracy said he was hooked and really wanted to go again.

Interests

When I heard that story I told Ralphene that I really wanted to take Luke fishing. Last Friday, I was planning to play poker with some friends, and then go with Ralphene to Vacaville to watch Bella Vista wrestle on Saturday. About 3 pm on Friday we got a call from Tracy, and he told Ralphene that he and Luke could go fishing on Saturday (I had offered to go anytime) so I couldn't say no. Truthfully, I was not looking forward to fishing since I was 0 for 31 times salmon fishing this year.

Once I got in the car, met Luke, and started talking old times with Tracy, those feelings vanished, and I had a great time.

Tracy had not done much fishing, so he had not taken Luke, except that one time with Todd. We began by dropping anchor and spinner fishing for salmon. Salmon fishing had been terrible for me the previous 31 days, and this day was proving no better. After hours of sitting there and not one pulldown, I decided we would troll for them. I changed to sardine-wrapped flatfish and different-colored spinners, but no luck. We had been fishing for five hours and not one bite. I am sure Luke thought before the day started that here was the great guide (Coach Lee) who his dad had bragged about as being a great fisherman, and he expected to catch a 49-pound salmon. NOTHING. But during that entire time he had not complained once and continued to hold the rod in his hands 90% of the time, since I had told him at the first of the day that you had a better chance of catching a fish if you were holding the rod.

It was about time for us to leave, but I wanted him to catch a fish. He had been such a trooper. We went to Dead Man's Slough, a small body of water just above the confluence of the Feather and Sacramento Rivers. We slowly motored up the slough for about 1/4 mile, having to to be careful since it was shallow and full of logs. Once tied off with our brush-grabber (do not feel right now like explaining for non-fisher people), we baited and almost immediately got a bite. Luke just lit up! This is what he came for. Forget about those 49-pound salmon. He wanted action! He proceeded to get 11 quick bites in 11 casts. He was on the ALERT. Just let him land one. And then there it was—he hooked and landed a beautiful ten-inch channel catfish. It was well worth the whole day of no bites to see his face. It was time to go, but he had caught his first catfish. Can't wait to take him again. Forget about those salmon—we are heading for DEAD MAN'S SLOUGH!

Temporary Insanity

I am sure most of you have done something, that upon reflection, you would not do again. I have three memories of things that I have done, that I would not have done had I been in my right mind. The only reason I could give was temporary insanity.

Spell #1 My friend Barry Rannells and I were on a trout fishing trip to the Trinity River in Northern California. We stopped at a fish hatchery to see the trout that were swimming in a rather large pool below a wing dam. There were some real MONSTERS, maybe up to 10 pounds or more. Barry kept saying what a thrill it would be to hook into a trout like that. We were on the last day of our fishing trip, and it was what I would consider a fair trip, having caught many trout—nothing over 12 inches. In those days we were looking for big trout. Barry kept saying, "Man, look at the size of those fish!" Before I knew what was happening, I had my spinning rod out with a large mepps spinner attached to the end of my line and was casting to those trout. Now there were two large signs that read "Fish Hatchery—NO FISHING!" The Department of Fish and Game office was right across the pool, maybe 50 yards away. And nothing to obstruct the view of anyone foolish enough to try fishing.

Sure enough, before I had made a second cast, a car came racing across the road. I did not really notice until Barry started running down the bank, heading for the woods. By the time I came to my senses, the warden had me. Caught dead to rights. Rod in hand with lure attached. He did not say a word, just took my rod, cut off my lure, (evidence) before giving me a citation for $150, which I paid by mail so as not to have to show up in a Trinity County Courthouse. I would have pled temporary insanity!

Spell #2 My dad started taking me duck and goose hunting at Tule Lake when I was 12 years old. I fell in love with the place. It was some of the best duck hunting and goose hunting in the entire

U.S. I continued to hunt there for the next 55 years. My brother and several friends hunted with me. I saw the hunting get worse and worse by the year, for several reasons. The main reasons were the lack of breeding grounds in Canada (reducing the number) plus the Fish and Game started feeding the birds on the refuge. Anyhow, the hunting got tougher. There were so many birds on the refuge, just out of reach.

On a foggy morning my friend Barry Rannells (again), Dick Cristofani, and I started out with goose decoys in hand to do a little goose hunting. It was so foggy I could hardly make out the sign "Upper Tule Lake Wild Life Refuge ABSOLUTELY NO HUNTING." I did not mention that sign to Barry or Dick.

We set our decoys out in the fog, built our blind of cut straw, and waited for light. As the light came and the fog started to clear, we began to have the best hunting you could imagine. Dick was killing honkers with his 16-gauge shotgun. The ducks were even flying by at house height. What a day. We were about out of ammo and had enough shooting for anyone.

Barry said he needed to relieve himself, and walked over to a dike about 30 yards away. He came running back and shouted, "My God, we're in the middle of the refuge!" Had we been caught, we would still be in the poky. I would plead Temporary Insanity again.

Spell #3 I am parked in the lot on the lower Tule Lake Wild Life Refuge. I am parked right in front of the refuge sign, behind a fence and about 40 yards in front of "no man's land," a strip of bare ground between the fence and the marsh on the refuge. The ducks are all over the place. I have hunted the open land all day and not even had one shot. The sight of all those ducks just yards away pushed me over the edge. I took my gun and made for the middle of the refuge. Just as I was about to kill my first mallard, I heard the sound of the ranger's green truck. As I ducked down in the marsh grass, the ranger pulled up beside my truck and began to glass the marsh with his binoculars. I stayed hunkered down in the wet weeds for what seemed like hours. He finally left, and I made a beeline for my truck and the safety of Carmichael. Temporary Insanity again.

One and Only Duck Hunting Trip
by Ralphene

When Charlie and I were dating that first fall in Iowa City, he was gone a lot during hunting season. I didn't quite get it, and I guess I must have complained about it, so he offered to take me along so I could appreciate what hunting was all about. His best friend, Mark Manders, was his hunting companion. The two of them had a hunting trip planned for a Sunday morning after a Saturday home football game. Charlie invited me to go along.

Now first of all, we had to go EARLY to get situated in the fields when the ducks would be coming in. He said he would pick me up at 5 am. This is on a Sunday morning! I had to sneak out a side door of the dorm where he and Mark were waiting for me in his little Chevy Impala. I had on jeans and a sweater and a warm jacket, and I thought I was ready.

We get to the field and get out of the car. Charlie and Mark are decked out in their hunting gear, and Charlie had a waterproof poncho for me to wear. He put it over my head and it draped around my ankles. (Oh yes, perfect hunting weather—pouring down rain!) So off we go. First, we have to climb over a barbed wire fence. Someway the guys managed to get me over the fence in my huge poncho. We walked what seemed like miles. When we reach a certain spot right in the middle of the field, Charlie says, "Lie down on your belly here, and don't get up. We'll be back soon." So I do, and off the guys go. Well, I don't know how long I laid there in the rain in that muddy field. I know it was a couple hours. Finally the two of them come back—all smiles. They had three ducks! I was so mad I could hardly talk.

To make it worse, we got back to the dorm at just the time many girls were coming out the door with their boyfriends, all dressed up and heading to church. And I was a wet muddy mess sneaking in the side door. Charlie never did understand why I didn't want to go hunting with him again!

The Coat

One chilly fall day Ralphene and David had gone somewhere (I don't remember where), so I decided to go pheasant hunting. Susie was about six or seven years old, and I thought she might like to go hunting with her dad.

Sure enough, she did, but now for the clothing. I got her into a pair of blue jeans, some warm socks, and old boots. Now for the coat. The only thing I could find was a good-looking tan coat hanging in the coat closet. Bundled Susie up in the coat and off we went after some pheasants. Hunting was just fair. I think I got one bird after about three or four hours of tramping through the brambles and brush. Susie was a real trooper—she plowed right along with me, getting the tan coat full of brambles.

When we got home, Ralphene had a fit. The coat was a special cashmere coat my mother had had custom-made by a seamstress. I was in the doghouse!

Miscellaneous Memories, February 15, 2005

I'm typed out. I don't know whether to thank or to blame Targe Lindsay for getting me into this. I must admit, it has caused me to think about a great many experiences. Some of the Montana fishing trips (although not connected with wrestling) bring back some fond memories. The trip to Calgary with Barry and Roy. (Could not tell all.) I thought about the Montana trip with Bruce and David, another trip with David and me and Bruce Summers and little Bruce. David and I on our trip to Lake of the Woods for a week, where we saw an 80-year old man fly fishing from a canoe (with his father). They were the talk of the backcountry. The countless trips with my partner Bill Hickey when we ran the Charliebill Guide Service. My first experience with White Horse Rapids (damn you, Hickey). You had me so frightened I almost wet my pants. That trip alone would take as many pages as these wrestling memoirs. The family trips to Iowa every summer (to Poverty Knob) with stops at the Grand Canyon and Yellowstone (when you could pull over anywhere and camp and wet your line). Ennis, Sheridan, Bozeman, Calgary, Grants Pass, Elko, Mt. Pleasant, Iowa City, Houston, Las Vegas, Hawaii, Vancouver Island, Campbell River, Gold River, Cody Wyoming, Dillon, Dell, Wise River, Last Chance, Ponds Lodge, Medford, Dunsmuir, Mt. Shasta—each with a story.

The Madison, Big Hole, the Skunk, Firehole, Sheep Creek, the Jefferson, the Smith, the Conway, the Boulder, Lewiston, Rogue, Salt, Upper Sacramento, the Delta, Tugboat Adventures, the Hoe, Mossy Creek, the Yellow Breeches, the Colorado, the Green around Pinedale, the Wise, the Gallatin, the Rappahannock, flies, black plastic, the pond (fall), the phantom bass, the mystery cutthroat, Eagle Rock, Kyberz, BC ferries, favors, Quadra Island honeys, Bill's recipe, Fletcher and the Sheepherder, me, Bruce S. and Dick C. in Elko (shut it down), Roy's birthdays on the road, reunions, Lucky Derby, Phoenix, Rounders, Red Lion, Stockman, Silver $ Bar (back room), Trumps 100-200, Dunsmuir (cold-decked), Capitol Casino, Reno, Tunica, South Dakota (on the reservation), Bayshore 101, San Pablo, college poker game (won a car), the local floating game (20 years), Vince, Barry Alan, Police, ice water, glasses broken, Barry Rannells, (too many to count). I have vivid memories of experiences on all of the above-mentioned. It would take too long to explain each, and only a few people would appreciate them.

Poker chip given at Charlie's Memorial Service
on December 28, 2010.

Charlie Lee on Texas Hold-em
Advice to David when he asked
his dad about Texas Hold-em
February 27, 2005

You can beat poker on the internet—if you follow these instructions absolutely—to the letter. It's too late for you to be thinking about playing in a real card club. Just take my word for it, unless you just want to do it a couple of times a year. Print these instructions and have them with you when you play until you become totally familiar with them.

Texas Hold-em: $2-$4 limit or $1-$2.

Absolutely do not ever play any higher. On the internet, only play in ten-handed games—or maybe nine.

When you are **first to act** (right after the big blind), only play these hands: AA-KK-QQ, AK suited.

2nd: As above, plus JJ, 10/10, AK, AQ suited, and KQ suited.

3rd: All of the above, plus 9/9, 8/8, AJ suited.

4th: As above, plus A/10 suited, KJ suited, QJ suited, 7/7, 6/6.

5th: (7th after the flop.) Above, plus KQ, A-9, suited, A-5 suited, (which I would prefer, because of the possibility of the straight). Play the 9 because of position. If a nine comes, the A is the best kicker. K/10 suited, J/10 suited, KJ.

6th: (after big blind) All of the above, plus 10/9 suited, J/10, 5/5, 4/4.

7th: add 9/8 suited and 8/7 suited, 3/3, 2/2.

8th: (you are the dealer) All of the above, plus once every 10 rounds, when you are dealing, RAISE with none of the above, raise with 2/4 suited, 5/6 suited, 7/6 off-suit, K/7 suited—anything you like, and if you do not hit a flop—Drop.

9th: (you are the small blind) If someone has opened ahead of you, only come in with AA, KK, QQ, AK suited—that is it—and RAISE. If no one has come in ahead of you, you must have: AA, KK, QQ, JJ, 10/10, AK suited, KQ suited, AJ suited, A/10 suited, J/10 suited, and you must raise every time that situation comes up. If you are raised, raise back with AA, KK, QQ. Just call with the other hands.

10th: (you are the big blind) If no one has raised, check and see the flop. Raise, only with AA, KK, or AK suited. If there is a raise ahead of you, call with AA, KK, QQ, AK suited, KQ suited, KJ suited, J/10 suited—nothing else. In the above hands, if someone has raised ahead of you, re-raise with AA or KK. Call only with QQ, AK suited, AQ suited, KQ suited.

That's it—unless you are the dealer, then call with the above hands plus, JJ, 10/10, 9/9, 8/8, AQ unsuited, KQ unsuited, and AJ suited.

So much for what hands to play. Now for a couple of little things that you must do. Remember to look for ten-handed games, but it is OK to play nine-handed if you have to, but use the same rules.

Keep track of your opponents' names so you do not play with the same people too often, as they will soon get a line on your play and will tighten up their opening play against you and will give you little action. This should not be too hard when you play at Party Poker, as they have thousands of players.

Open up an electronic account to coincide with your bank account. Open with $400. This is absolutely all the money you will be willing to lose. Buy $100 in the 2-4 game.

Critical: Play a maximum of three hours—not one minute more. When you get $50 ahead, you must QUIT.

Do not play again for 24 hours.

So you can never play more than once a day for more than three hours.

If you lose all $400 in four settings you are DONE. Go surfing, but $400 is enough to overcome short-range bad bets (and they surely will happen).

Remember, you are trying to make money, period. Do not think about having fun.

You have to be like a programmed robot. You must do EXACTLY as outlined each and every hand. Get the requirements in your head and follow them.

David's response to his dad's advice

OK, perfect. That's the info I need to give it a go sometime. For starters, I may go to Bay 101 just for the experience of it. I've only played at a public poker table twice. Keep going where you left off—Thanks, D

Charlie's reply

You said you might try the Bay 101. You should still use the program, although it will take a while for you to memorize proper play. The problem with a card club is that they will soon get a line on this style of play, and they will tighten up their playing requirements and give you little action. Remember, you are trying to make money, period. Don't think about having fun or being a good guy who likes to socialize. (Go play hearts if you want that.)

I have told other young players over the years about this strategy. That was before internet play. Not one could stay with it. It should be much easier to play on the computer. It is boring and tedious, but after you have banked that first $1,000, it will become more interesting. Keep me posted. Any questions? Love, Dad

Another Question by David
By Ralphene

Just a few years ago we were watching The World Series of Poker in our living room. It is not surprising that this was a favorite pastime of Charlie and David. (I must admit, for a few years, I really enjoyed it too!)

One night, David said to his dad, "Dad, what's the biggest pot you ever won in a poker game?" Charlie calmly replied, "A Chrysler Imperial." So here's the story, or what I recall of it.

When we were newlyweds and still college students living in Iowa City, Charlie and I would often spend weekends in Mt. Pleasant with my folks. We would drive up the hill to Poverty Knob on fumes, and fill the gas tank from the big barrel by the garage. It was great to have a Sinclair oilman for a dad! My mom would always have Charlie's favorites in the fridge and would prepare meals fit for a king. I think her picnic hampers full of fried chicken, homemade potato salad, deviled eggs, etc. might have been what sealed the deal for me!

Charlie soon learned that there was a Friday night poker game at the VFW in town. He also quickly figured out that there were some pretty wealthy farmers who played in that game. Any opportunity he had, he would visit the VFW Friday night card game and usually came home with some extra money. On this particular occasion, he came home driving a Chrysler Imperial! I don't remember the model year, but the car was black, with a green swoop on the side. He won it in the card game at the VFW!

Well, R. E. Ward, as he was known to the townspeople, was not happy about his son-in-law playing in the game to begin with. You can imagine how he felt about the Chrysler! I did not hear the conversation, but I do know that Charlie never played in the VFW game again. However, we did drive a pretty sweet Chrysler for a couple years!

Footnote: I do not know what Charlie put up against that car. I did not ever want to ask!!

Once Was Enough (Your Eyes Only)
Obviously this was meant only for Targe!

When we left breakfast this morning, Barry Alan told me he really enjoyed himself. It was good to see Kenny and Cody. Barry told me to have a safe trip back, and asked if I was going to play in the big game again. I told him, "Once was enough!" Over the years I had saved $50,000 which I kept in $100 bills in a large safe in our family room. When we traveled to D.C., I took it along in a pouch that I never let out of my sight. We had stopped for the night in Nebraska and gotten up early for breakfast. After breakfast we drove about 150 miles and stopped at Cabela's Sporting Goods Store to shop around and buy a few presents. (This was one of our regular stops when we went back the central route.) Ralphene was doing some shopping, and I was trying on some waders, when I suddenly realized that I didn't have my money pouch! (I know you are thinking, "How could you forget that?") I break into a cold sweat. I'm thinking maybe Ralphene has it. I quickly hunt her up, but no pouch.

Now we were both starting to panic. I told her to go check the car. I feel terrible. She came back and said it was not in the van. We agreed that we had it when we left the motel, and the only place we stopped was the spot for breakfast. I said I was positive I took it in when we went for breakfast. I guess I must have left it sitting in the restaurant booth. I was trying to think if we should call and see if they found a pouch. But then I think, if they find it, they will probably look inside. I was not sure I wanted to trust their honesty, so we decided to just drive back and take our chances.

There is a silence you could cut with a knife on the way back to the van. Ralphene had told me not to carry that kind of money with us. I knew she was right. But she never said, "I told you so." When we got back to the van, I found the pouch under a pile of clothes. Ralphene was so shook that when she went to look, she didn't see it. Talk about relief!!

After that little side story, let me get back to my original thought. I had always wanted to play in the $10,000 buy-in no-limit hold-em World Championship in Las Vegas. But I never got around to it, mainly because I did not want to pony up the 10K. Ralphene told me to go ahead—(with my sock money, of course). So I had her blessing. How many wives could you say that about? The main reason I didn't play in the World Series is because I made such good money playing in the side games.

The only poker they have around Washington, D.C. is about five hours away in Atlantic City. We decide to take a couple of days off from grandkid-watching and go there. I make reservations at Trump's place and off we go. I wanted to take a shot at making some real $. I told Ralphene that I was going to get in the $50-$100 Hold-em game. Of course she had no idea what that was. She just said, "Win some $," and went up to the room to read a book. I walked into the poker room about 3 pm. There were about 25-30 tables going. I went to the high-limit section and asked the floorman if there was a seat in the 50-100 game. There was no seat, so he put me in a 15-30 game and asked me if I wanted to be on the $100-200 list. I said sure, not really having any intention of actually playing in that game.

Family poker game while on vacation at the Bar Lazy J Guest Ranch in Colorado.

About ten minutes later I hear, "Lee, your 1 & 2 seat is open." Now, I know I am not supposed to play in that game, but I have $20,000 cash in my pocket, so here goes. I bought $10,000 in chips and pulled up a seat. The 1-2 game gets your full attention real quick. About two hours into the game "CHIPS" brought me another rack. Now I am in the game for $20,000. I lost another

$2,000. I was not feeling too good about now. I was in the big blind, and one player bought in for a raise, and one guy calls. I called 200, and the first bettor raised and the second raiser killed it. I looked down and saw a 4-6 of hearts. I called the 200. There are four of us in for 400 each. The flop was 5 diamonds, ace of diamonds, king of hearts. I was first to act. Check, the next two guys checked, the last man bet 100. I was hot and stuck, so I thought I would just call this hundred and see what happened. I called, the first guy re-raised, the next guy called, and the last guy killed it again. Now they trap me. I made a bad call and threw in another 200. $3,200 in the pot. The turn card was the seven of clubs. I picked up an open-ended straight, but you can lose a lot of money chasing hands like that. I checked, the first guy bet 200. Here we go again. It got killed a third time. Now we have $6,400 in the pot. I was praying to the Poker God for a 3 or an 8 and no diamond. 3 OF HEARTS on the river. I checked. Bet 200, fold, raise 200, I called 400, raise, re-raise, I call 400 more with the PURE NUTS. The first player had pocket kings, the next guy the nut flush draw, and the last guy had pocket aces. I won a $7,600 pot and ended up getting my $12,000 back, plus $3,800 profit. BUT ONCE IS ENOUGH!

A Lesson For the Kid

I had Ralphene drop me off at the Phoenix Casino yesterday, March 2, 2010. I had to wait for about 15 minutes to get a seat, as all games were full. A seat opened in the 5-10 Omaha game so I took it. I only played two hands when a seat in the 4-8 Hold-em game opened up. I took it because Omaha is not my favorite game. I had been playing for about an hour and was stuck $40 when the daily tournament was announced. I paid the $40 entry fee and took a seat. You received $5,000 in tournament chips, and the game started. It was a re-buy game, and after only 35 minutes I was broke. I decided not to re-buy, so kiss that $40 goodbye. A seat was open in the $2-$3 no limit. I bought in for $500. Let the game begin. After an hour and a half I was down $150, so I put my name up for the 4-8 Hold-em game.

Things soon began to look up. The cards ran for me. I was ahead $550 in about two hours. A very good win for that limit. Now for the reason for this story. Sometimes in poker, things happen that you enjoy, aside from winning money. This is one of those. I was in the 2 seat in a full 9-handed table. In the 8 seat was a kid who looked to be in his early twenties. He was stuck about $100 or so, much of which was in my stack. He was not only losing, but was also a poor loser. When I won a pot, he would announce, "The old man gets lucky again." I was on the dealer's button and held a 7 and 10 of hearts, not a very good hand, but I had been running lucky. The player after the big blind brings it on for a raise of $. The "kid" as I will call him, just calls. The original bettor caps the bet, so it costs each of us $16 to see the flop. The flop is 8 of hearts, 5 of hearts, jack of spades. The first man checked, the kid bet 4 bucks, I called with an inside straight draw, the first bettor folded. The turn was a king of spades, no help for me. The kid bets $8. I just called. The river comes, an ace of clubs. The kid bets out $8. I had nothing, so the only way I could win was to raise and hope he would fold. I raised, he did not hesitate, he raised. I thought sure I was beaten.

While I started to throw my hand away, he began talking. He says, "I made two pair." Why would he say anything? I re-raised and he mucked his cards. I showed my 7-10 of hearts. One of the players said, "He only has 10 high." Well, you could have lit a match on his rear, he was so hot. Some of the other players got on him and that made him hotter yet. Just about then Ralphene comes in to pick me up. I cashed in with an $859 win. On my way out, I looked at the kid and mouthed the words "THANK YOU" as we were going out the door. He yelled two words which I can't repeat. The last words were, "____, old man!"

Sweet Deal
by Ralphene

After Charlie's death, I needed to sell the handicapped-equipped Chrysler Town and Country van that had served us so well on all of our cross-country trips. Charlie said it rode like a stage coach, and I guess it did, but it carried his scooter, all our belongings for our six-month stay in Maryland, along with our German Shepherd, Freddie. It was a perfect vehicle for us, not to mention being perfect to haul three grandkids around. (And, it was purchased with sock money!!)

I decided to find a new vehicle before selling the Chrysler. I absolutely hate looking at cars and always left that part up to Charlie. So I talked to Bruce, Susie, David, and any friends who were knowledgeable about cars, seeking good advice.

A good friend asked if I had ever considered a salvaged vehicle. I had never even heard the term. I learned that this was a vehicle that had suffered damage in a collision and which would not be financially feasible to repair. So these vehicles were fixed up and sold for a much cheaper price—and it was "buyer beware." My friend said that he had purchased several salvaged cars over the years, and he had no regrets about any of them.

I mentioned the idea of a salvaged vehicle to Bruce, and his very words were, "Don't even think about that, Redhead." And I always respect Bruce's opinion. Next I mentioned the idea to my good friend Sharon, who was in charge of leasing cars for a large company for 25 years, and REALLY KNOWS CARS! Her answer was, "I wouldn't touch one with a ten-foot pole!" OK.

Well, my friend was scanning the newspapers for used vehicles, and he called me one day to tell me he read about a nice Honda CRV that sounded good. I told him I had almost decided against taking a chance on a salvaged vehicle, but my friend made this car sound so good that I thought, "What the heck. Can't hurt to take a look." So, this friend of mine contacted the owner who happened to be a young Russian kid in his early twenties. We agreed to meet at the Costco parking lot the next day. On arriving at Costco, we were pleasantly surprised to see a sweet-looking sky-blue CRV at the designated meeting spot. I couldn't believe it. Now I really wanted that car! The kid was the driver, and a woman was in the passenger's seat. She turned out to be his mother and was apparently supervising the operation.

We all went for a drive, my friend driving and the two owners in the back seat conversing rapidly in Russian! After 15 minutes or so we returned to Costco. We agreed that the kid would meet us the next day at my 76 garage on the corner near my house. Ray, the mechanic there, has taken care of our cars for years. In the meantime, I ran a Carfax on the vehicle and saw that, yes, it had been declared totaled, and there was front-end and frame damage. I took the report to Ray and asked him if he would check the car out for me the next day, which he agreed to do.

We meet the next day. Ray puts the car on the hoist, examines it carefully, and all looks good. The owner of the station takes the car for a drive on the freeway for me, all good there. Now we need to agree on a price. (Of course, Mom is along too. The kid is obviously learning the ropes.) Blue book at the time was $21,000. (This was a loaded car with leather seats, navigation system, back-up camera, etc.) After some negotiation, I ended up getting it for $11,500. A couple of little things needed to be fixed first, which the kid agreed to. (We are sure he took it to his Russian cousin who probably repaired it in the first place!)

Long story short, I ended up with a sweet vehicle, with a perfect spot in the back for Nala, my German Shepherd. It drives like a dream. I LOVED the car then, and I still do.

I could tell you another little story about a future encounter with my Russian friend, but that is for another time!! My good friend had the time of his life with this escapade. If I ever need another car, TL is my man!

When my friends ask me how the heck I could take such a gamble on a car, my answer is, "How could I be married for almost fifty years to Charlie Lee and not take a risk on such a sweet deal?"

Food!

Food has played an important role in my life. My favorite meal, I guess, would be my grandmother's chicken and dumplings. She passed away over 50 years ago, but I still can remember going to the little house they rented in Fair Oaks and having her fix that special dish. Yum!

I think about the Hamburger Inn in Iowa City. For 23 cents you could buy the best burger ever. I would buy five burgers and they would last me the whole walk across the river and back to my dorm from a movie downtown.

When McDonald's came to town, I used to take Ralphene out for a cheap date. For 70 cents we would get two hamburgers, two orders of french fries, and two Cokes. My first luxury meal was at the Inn at Little Washington in Virginia. Don't remember what we had, but I do know it cost $250. We also tried the French Laundry in the Napa Valley. It was along the same line as the Inn at Little Washington. Those are good for a once-in-a-lifetime experience, but I would not care to spend that much money on a meal again.

I recall our early trips to the Madison River in Montana, where I started the yearly tradition of buying steaks for the camp to celebrate Roy's birthday. I would drive to the butcher shop in Ennis and have him cut six to ten steaks, depending on how many guys showed up that year. The steaks would be cut 2 1/2 inches thick and be about the size of a large dinner plate. I would cook them myself on a hot wood fire on an outdoor grill. That was mighty good eating. Nobody ever offered to share the cost, and I never asked.

I never thought I'd eat again after going with my roommates to Bill Zuber's Dugout in the Amana Colonies. Bill Zuber had played for the New York Yankees. He was a big Hawkeye supporter. He would bring out pickled ham and beets and cottage cheese and sauerkraut and pickled beans. Then would come platters of fried chicken and mashed potatoes with the best gravy. We would top it off with apple strudel and ice cream. You could have as much as you wanted. In those days, at age 19, I could put away lots of chow. They would have to roll us out to our car, and we would all swear we would never eat again.

I made the baseball team my freshman year, and we took the train to play a series of games in Arizona. Zuber made the trip with the team and brought along more food than you could ever imagine. We ate like kings and went 0-5-1.

Ralphene and I spent five years in Washington, D.C. to be close to our grandkids. I think we spent most of the time eating. There are some great eateries in the D.C. area and we hit most of them. Now that we are back in California, we eat out almost every day for lunch, and usually at a different place each time. Many of our favorites are gone—the Coral Reef, one of the Hof Braus, the Nut Tree, and many others that I cannot recall.

Two hamburgers tie for first among memorable burgers. One of them was at a small drive-in in Markleeville, California. I had completed a five-day hike in the Desolation Wilderness area with a scout troop, during which time we survived on dehydrated food. Yuck! When we hit civilization, I headed straight for the burger place. The next time was when we crossed the Mexico/United States border after having spent two weeks in Mexico City watching David wrestle in the World Schoolboy Tournament. We hit the first McDonald's we saw, and that burger tasted like it came straight from Heaven.

When I played football for Iowa, one of the big perks was to make the traveling squad, which consisted of the first three teams, or 33 players. It was truly something—a complete smorgasbord. We always had steak and a fish dish and more sides than you could ever imagine. There are many more places, but I will have to get to them later. My typing finger just gave out.

Eating out in D.C.
By Ralphene

One thing Charlie and I really enjoyed, whether in Maryland or California, was eating out. I must say, Charlie was a true gourmet when it came to food, and he loved to tell how he "expanded my palate." True, I was an Iowa girl who grew up on meat and potatoes! When we took off on one of our frequent dining excursions, sometimes we had a reservation, but quite often, we did not. In fact, very often Charlie would just say, "Get in the car," and I would have no idea where we were going. It might have been to a Five Star restaurant—we enjoyed the French Laundry on one occasion, although one had to have a reservation well in advance for that. I never figured out how he swung that one. Sometimes we just went on a trip to a dive. We enjoyed them all!

We especially enjoyed experiencing the dining in the Washington, D.C./Bethesda area, which was very new to us when we moved there for our first six-month stay. Again, Charlie could always pick the places. I don't know how the heck he did it. Often they were in the news or just famous. We loved Ben's Chili Bowl and the Inn at Little Washington about equally. It was just fun to be together.

One particular trip I remember was one of those times Charlie said, "Get in the car. We're going to a little place I know." So we start out through our Rockville neighborhood. We had been driving fifteen minutes or so, and the surroundings were beginning to change considerably. By now I made sure the windows were rolled up and the doors were locked! Lots of graffiti on fences, row houses in not-very-good shape, broken windows. Finally, we pull into the parking lot of this little white building, slightly run-down. We go in, and the waitress seats us and gives us menus. Well, Charlie had always had a love of soul food, and this was just the place for him! He would usually order neckbones, greens, sweet potato pie, stuff like that. Those waitresses would LOVE taking care of him, calling him "Honey," etc. And of course he could really put the food away. He was their kind of guy!! Me, it was always a struggle to find something on the menu that I even wanted to order!

Well, Charlie was working on a second helping of everything, and in walks this very dapper-looking gentleman. He is wearing a cashmere overcoat and proceeds to take a seat on a stool at the counter in the back. As he works his way back, we hear the servers and cooks say, "Good afternoon, Your Honor." It was Clarence Thomas! We were at the Florida Grille, which is located behind the White House, in a not-so-good neighborhood. Turns out this is the favorite eatery of quite a group of rather famous Washingtonians, including Janet Reno. Now how the heck did Charlie know about that place??

I Should Have Seen That One Coming!
By Ralphene

After our kids were gone, I began to attend a few concerts at ARCO Arena with friends, rarely with Charlie. He and I did not exactly share a taste for the same type of music!

Neil Diamond was coming to town. In those days, he was a big name. I asked Charlie if he wanted to go. (Or rather, if he WOULD go with me.) To my surprise, he said he would. So we enjoyed the evening together, and it was fun. A few weeks later he said, "There is a prizefight in Reno next weekend that I really want to see. Want to go?" I said, "No thanks," and of course he said, "But I went to that concert with you." So I gave in and we went to the prizefight.

A few weeks after that, he mentioned a gun show in the Bay Area. Again, not something I really wanted to do. Same story—"But I went to your concert with you!" So off we go to the gun show. Next I think it was an MMA match. Same story. That went on several more times. Man, he got a LOT of mileage out of one crummy Neil Diamond concert!

Something tells me I should have seen that one coming!

High Level Competition
By Ralphene

During our married years, Charlie and I probably attended more athletic competitions than most people ever dream of. We enjoyed all sports, but Charlie especially enjoyed watching ANY competition at the highest level. Whether it was a chess match, a horse show, croquet, whatever—if it was for all the marbles, it was always exciting to watch. I remember when Charlie first told me we were going to drive to the Bay Area to watch a high school football team play (the legendary De La Salle of Concord). I thought he was nuts, but I went along. And did I ever love it! We watched them play several times, but the time I remember most was a game that was broadcast on ESPN. De La Salle was playing a nationally-ranked out-of-state opponent, and it was a BIG game. So we got there early. Parked in the parking lot and watched ESPN bring in their big trucks and cameras and set up to broadcast the game. Charlie had his scooter, so he was buzzing around, talking to all the sportscasters, the coaches, etc. I mostly sat in our van or in the bleachers reading and waiting for the game to start.

Now it is almost game time, and Charlie knows where I am sitting. But did he join me? Heck no, he was right behind the De La Salle bench on his scooter for the whole game!

During the years we lived part-time in Maryland, we grew to really appreciate sports as they were played on the East Coast. We became lacrosse fans—a sport that was rarely heard of in California at the time. Our granddaughters played lacrosse at their junior high school, so that was especially fun to watch, but we would also go to the city high school championships as well.

We had a particular interest in basketball, since both grand-daughters were pretty talented youngsters on the basketball court. Alex's AAU coach also coached an elite high school team in the area, so we would follow Good Counsel, even though we had no one playing there yet. It got so we followed teams enough that we would go to the Washington, D.C. high school city play-offs at the end of the season—boys and girls.

I especially remember one boys' championship game, held in a very old high school in the middle of downtown D.C. We went early and had to park a mile from the school. Charlie had his scooter, so that made things much simpler. At those games, the rival teams would often have gang associations, so there was intense security. Metal detectors were brought in, and security was as tight as any airport line I have ever been through. You had hundreds of people in line waiting to get in. On this particular evening, we had waited in line for at least an hour outside, and this was not a happy crowd. So when we finally got through security, I was very relieved. I followed the throng, and there were virtually NO seats to be found in this huge two-decker gym. By now I realize I have lost Charlie. Not much chance of even finding him in here, and in those days, we had cell phones, but they would not get reception in a building like this, and texting was unheard of. So I figure he is in here someplace and sooner or later I will spot him. Or at least we will meet up outside when the game is over. (Those of you who know me, realize I could never have gotten back to our car on my own, not in a million years!) So I take a seat way up high in the balcony, crammed amidst a group of noisy fans. I am not real happy about now. I look all around, and sure enough, there he is, sitting right in the middle of the press row, court-side, the row that has a table in front so the sportscasters can use their laptops or notebooks or whatever. Of course he has a press pass on a lanyard around his neck, AND a spiral notebook in hand. That was vintage Charlie! (As you might imagine, he pulled the same stunt on several other occasions as well!)

FAMILY

Family
By Ralphene

No one was more of a family man than Charlie. His kids and grandkids were his life. No one could ask for a better husband, father, or grandfather.

While this book does not focus on family stories as such, an entire volume could be written about his family. While we had always been a large part of our grandkids' lives, we had the good fortune to become even more involved with them when we lived part-time in Maryland for five years. We attended their soccer games, baseball games, softball games, basketball games, lacrosse matches, and track meets. We were spectators at the Pinewood Derby and many Boy Scout Ceremonies, as well as Norwood School concerts, assemblies, and drama productions. Gramps loved to take his grandkids out to "paint the town" and boy did the kids enjoy those excursions! Those memories will last forever.

Charlie was instrumental in starting our annual family vacations. The first one was to The Power House in 1997, a famous landmark structure outside of Ennis, Montana. The Power House had its own fishing pond, well-stocked with large trout, with a stream running behind it, connecting to the small creek that led to the Madison, and of course the Madison River itself, just a walk across the meadow. The home was beautifully furnished and appointed in a western theme. We returned to the Power House in the summer of 1999. Charlie found this wonderful place in the days before internet searches were known—at least to him.

We continued this family tradition each year, with vacations to many exciting locations, such as a week at the Bar Lazy J Guest Ranch in Parshall, Colorado, a surfing week in Santa Cruz, and a trip to the Rose Bowl when Wisconsin played Stanford in 2000. Each year all nine of us would get together for at least a week, and sometimes longer. Wonderful times! We continue the tradition still, although it has become increasingly difficult with young adults in college, beginning married life, and embarking on careers.

If Charlie were around today, I know he would be working on a volume called "The Special Three!"

A Grandfather's Legacy
By Susie Lee Stadnik, written on December 8, 2010

"Grandfather's Legacy" was a late night impromptu response to my request before Charlie's Memorial, asking for insight into the lessons Charlie taught his grandkids. Quick, succinct, and insightful, this summary suggests that these lessons were well-taught and well-learned by more than one generation.

—Targe Lindsay

He taught them how to fish, play chess, and play poker.

He taught them the importance of family and what it means to have unconditional love and support.

He taught them that it's more interesting to play a game for a favor than just for fun.

He taught them how to be fierce competitors and how to win and lose with dignity.

He taught them to work hard and never miss a practice.

He taught them to always be on time.

He taught them to expand their palate and try new foods and new life experiences.

He taught them what it means to have character, determination, and bravery, and how to face adversity with grace and style.

He taught them how to persevere without complaining and to always do their best.

He taught them that in life you have to play the hand you're dealt.

Sam, Matt, Susie, and Alex at Matt's 2014 Stanford Graduation.

Family

Timeline of the Life of Charlie Lee

February 16, 1939	Born in Omaha, Nebraska
1946	Family moves to Waseca, Minnesota
May 1, 1946	Brother Bruce is born
1950	Lee family heads to California
June 1956	Graduates from San Juan High School
August 1956	Enters University of Iowa
January 1959	Iowa wins Rose Bowl
Spring of 1959	Charlie and Ralphene meet
December 10, 1960	Charlie and Ralphene marry in Mt. Pleasant, Iowa
Dec. 1960-Jan. 1961	Honeymoon: signs with Houston Oilers; plays in Copper Bowl, All American Bowl, and Hula Bowl
June 1961	Charlie and Ralphene graduate from Iowa University
July 1961	Attends Houston Oilers training camp
August 1961	Attends Central Missouri State College; Serves as line coach
June 1962	Receives Master of Science in Education from Central Missouri State College
August 1962	Begins teaching at Bella Vista High School; coaches football and wrestling
May 8, 1963	Daughter Susie is born
May 24, 1966	Son David is born
1977	Super Stars Wrestling Club is formed
1979	Chosen as Scholastic Wrestling News National Wrestling Coach of the Year
June 1981	Susie graduates from Bella Vista High School
June 1984	David graduates from Bella Vista High School
June 1985	Susie graduates from Stanford University
August 1, 1987	Susie marries Andrew Stadnik
May 2, 1990	Granddaughter Alexandra Lee Stadnik is born
June 1990	David graduates from Stanford
June 5, 1992	Grandson Matthew Charles Stadnik is born
June 9, 1994	Retires from Bella Vista High School
July 18, 1994	Granddaughter Samantha Rae Stadnik is born
2001	Inducted into California Wrestling Hall of Fame
2002-2007	Charlie and Ralphene live in Maryland six months of the year
Sept. 9, 2010	Dies in Carmichael, California at age 71
2012	Inducted into Sac-Joaquin Section Athletic Hall of Fame
	Alex graduates from Southern Utah University; interns at Stanford
	Sam enters Santa Clara University
January-March 2013	Alex works as strength and conditioning coach for wrestlers at Bella Vista while completing her master's thesis
2013	Alex receives Master's Degree in Sports Conditioning and Performance from Southern Utah University; interns with Olympic Ski and Snowboard team in Park City, Utah
	Alex takes job as Strength and Conditioning Coach at BYU
June 2014	Matt graduates from Stanford University
June 20, 2014	Alex marries Tommy Gruenewald
June 2015	Sam graduates from Santa Clara University

Young Charlie with his mother, Florence Mae Lee.

Just Starting Out

I was born in Omaha, Nebraska on February 16, 1939. My mother was a stay-at-home mom all her life. My father was an iron worker by trade, but did whatever it took to provide (what he considered to be) a good standard of living for his family. When I was not yet four years old, we moved to Toledo, Ohio to live with my mother's parents, while my father and his two brothers, Clarence and Oscar, went to Iran during World War II to work as civilians in the oil fields.

I have scant memory of the two years we spent with my grandparents, Wally and Marie Young. I do remember that I thought I had the best of everything. My grandfather was an engineer on the Ohio railroad. We lived close enough that he could walk to work. They never owned a car or a house (always rented). My grandfather LOVED to fish. Almost every afternoon when he returned from work, we would walk down to Lake Erie for some catfishing. I remember him cooking some crawdads in a large soup can. He did not practice catch and release! We would take those catfish home.

In the basement he had a large board to which he would nail the catfish by the head, then skin it. He was a true expert at that. I spent a lot of time with my granddad, which meant I spent a lot of time fishing. My love for fishing definitely began there.

My grandmother (Marie Schultz) Young had spent many years in the employ of a very well-to-do family as their head cook. She was a genuine wizard in the kitchen. I think that was where I developed my fondness for a good meal and my love of cooking. Her chicken and dumplings served with liver balls was something special.

My mother was somewhat religious, and her mother was involved in several church activities, so my mom also got involved. She often tried to get my father to go to church, but he said he lived by the Golden Rule. He told me it would not be a bad idea if I did the same. I have always tried to live up to that advice.

My parents always treated everyone they met or knew with respect. I can not ever recall them saying anything derogatory about anyone behind their back. Not a bad legacy. My sense of how to treat people has probably not been hurt by living with a true saint for 46 years.

One day when I was eight years old, I was kind of bored with nothing much to do, so I decided to walk across the street to my friend's house with my eyes closed. I walked straight into a tree and knocked two front (permanent) teeth out. So for years, kids would tease me. It was a long time until I got that problem fixed permanently.

When the Lee brothers returned from three years in Iran, they were flush with cash. Clarence went looking for something to invest in. After what must have been three or four weeks, he came back with a plan to buy a block and tile company in Waseca, Minnesota. It was owned by a couple of tough old German brothers. So the entire tribe—my father and mother, my younger brother Bruce and I, Clarence, his wife Ruth, their two kids Bob and Karen, and Uncle Oscar moved to Waseca, Minnesota. My family moved into a two-bedroom apartment on the second floor over a saloon. Clarence, Ruth, Oscar, and the two kids took the middle apartment, just down a narrow dark hallway.

I really loved Waseca. I went to school in a true little two-room schoolhouse. There were only grades two through four, and 90% of the kids lived on farms. The town did everything for the kids—all sorts of sports teams, a wonderful lake. They would freeze the baseball diamond in the winter and have one huge skating rink.

We kids were always hunting something. Mainly helpless bluejays or crows. Always with our trusty Red Ryder pellet guns. My dad was very much a hunter. He was raised on a farm in South Dakota. He did not care for fishing, but I have fond memories of many hunting trips to Gayville, South Dakota for pheasants. Later, after we moved to California, I would go on some memorable hunts to Tule Lake in Northern California for ducks and geese. My father nurtured in me my love of hunting. I remember him going to great pains to always make sure he never let something he killed go to waste. That was a good lesson.

My mother loved Waseca and wanted my dad to build a house on the lake and make it our home. The Lee brothers had other plans. After three years, they turned the tile plant into a profit maker. They sold the business, and moved one block south and opened a factory that made a machine that produced irrigation pipe. After a year at that, they sold out and decided California was the place to be.

We loaded up the old green Pontiac, and Clarence packed up the Willies jeep, complete with trailer. We were off to the Golden State! I was excited, because I heard you could pick oranges right off the trees. The same for cherries and peaches. I could not wait!

We landed in Richmond, California and rented a small house. Nine people were too many, but I was used to sharing a room. The brothers had a hard time finding work in Richmond, but they were pretty well-heeled after selling out in Waseca. They took a few driving trips to get an idea of what might be available. They thought Sacramento looked promising, so they bought two lots in Arden Park and built two homes. The first home was made of cinderblock. That was the one nine of us moved into. Meanwhile, they built another home right next door. When the other house was finished, they sold it, and Clarence, Ruth, the two kids, and Uncle Oscar lived in the block house.

My dad bought a lot in Fair Oaks, where for $8,000 he built a great home. Bruce and I finally had our own room and nobody else was living in the house with us. My dad had joined the local iron workers' union, and was working steadily, but he wanted to earn more. He was fairly well-known and respected in those circles, and he landed a job as top foreman of civilian construction at Tule Air Base in Greenland. He was in Greenland off and on for four years. He made good money and was a happy man. I started my freshman year at El Camino, where I was cut from the freshman football team for missing a practice. I transferred to San Juan High School at the end of my freshman year, and I finished high school there.

I was a pretty fair athlete, and with the help of my history teacher, Joe Murtaugh, who had some connections with the Iowa football program, I was offered a full-ride scholarship to the University of Iowa. The Iowa coaching staff did this strictly on the word of Mr. Murtaugh. No film or scouting reports, nothing. I was also recruited by the Air Force Academy and the University of California at Berkeley. In addition, I was offered a professional baseball contract with the Pittsburg Pirates, which included a $3,000 signing bonus. That would buy a brand-new car in 1956. My parents made the decision for me, and I was off to Iowa.

My years at Iowa were the best of times. There were 105 freshmen football players on some form of scholarship. There were no limits in those days. Of that 105, only five of us graduated with a diploma. You could not play on the varsity as a freshman. There were 17 tackles on that freshman team. I never missed a practice in my entire career at Iowa, and I knew all my blocking assignments. At the start of my sophomore year, I was so far down on the depth chart that I was given #99. In those days the centers wore numbers in the 50s, guards in the 60s, tackles in the 70s, and ends in the 80s. So if your number was in the 90s, you were probably not going to play. There was another player who also had #99, and his name was listed in the program. As the season wore on, I moved rapidly up the depth chart. As I mentioned, I very seldom missed an assignment and since they did not have the platoon system then, (you had to go both ways) this meant you had better know your blocking assignments. Many of the players who started out ahead of me dropped by the wayside. By the fourth game I had made the traveling squad (which meant I went on all the road trips and ate at the training table). I played quite a lot. But every time I entered a game, I was introduced as the other player. That kind of bothered me, but turned out to be a blessing in disguise. That situation enabled me to have an extra year of eligibility.

Playing in the Rose Bowl and playing all the big-time teams, and always going first class, made for some memorable experiences. During the end of my junior year I met Ralphene. We courted for a couple of months, until school was out. I returned to California, and she stayed in Iowa for the summer. We picked up where we left off in the fall, and by the following November I asked her to marry me. We were going to get hitched in June, but I was drafted by the Houston Oilers and selected to play in the All-American Bowl in Tucson (Division I players vs Division II All-Americans). My team won. I also played in the Copper Bowl in Phoenix and from there on to the Hula Bowl. (My team also won both of those games.) This proved too good a honeymoon to pass up, so we moved the wedding up to December 10. Ralphene's mom was in a tizzy, but everything worked out. We had a wonderful black and gold wedding, and were gone 31 days. We came home with $11 more than we started out with!

Family History

I am going to try and put into print what I know of the Lee family history—the Lee side now, the Young side later, I hope.

My paternal grandfather came to the United States from Norway. I am not sure of the year. He arrived at Ellis Island and then traveled to Chicago by train. That was the end of the line. He walked from there to Gayville, South Dakota. He acquired a free section of land (640 acres). Free, as long as you stayed and developed it. He arrived with his first wife. I do not know her name. They lived in a sod house and burned cow chips for fuel. They had two children, Ralph and Marie.

His first wife died, and my grandfather married his housekeeper. He had become a fairly prosperous farmer by then. His name was Knute Olson when he arrived in the Gayville area, but there were so many Olsons, he changed his last name to Lee. He was considerably older than his wife Matilda. By the time he passed away, he and Matilda had five children—Zelma, Clarence, Oscar, Carrie, and my father, Charles. My father was two when his father died. His mother raised all five kids by herself.

Zelma (Sally) and Carrie (Tootie) attended South Dakota College and obtained nursing degrees. Oscar and Clarence did not go to college. My father started college with the intention of becoming a doctor, but because of some hard times that hit the family, he had to abandon that plan, and he dropped out of school. Tootie went to Omaha, Nebraska and got a nursing job which she had for 27 years. Sally got a nursing job in Laramie, Wyoming, which she had for 29 years. At the end of Tootie's nursing career in Omaha, she moved to Carmichael where she got a job at Sutter Memorial Hospital and worked as a head nurse for five years. After three years, Sally moved to Carmichael, and the sisters lived in a duplex that my father built for them. They stayed there for several years, then moved to an apartment in Carmichael where they lived until Tootie died. Sally then moved in with Clarence and his wife Ruth, until she passed away.

"Little Charlie" at age four in Toledo, Ohio
with his parents Florence and Charles.

Bruce and "Big Charlie" in the Arizona locker room in 1968
after a 14-7 victory over Wyoming with Bruce at quarterback.

Bruce

When people talk about their brothers, they either love 'em or hate 'em.

Bruce was born in Toledo, Ohio in 1946. I can still remember the day my mom and dad brought him home from the hospital in the back seat of our old green Chevy (Betsy).

I wondered to my mom, "How is he ever going to play with me when I am so much older?" My mom said not to worry, he would grow up, and "You both will have lots of fun together." Ma was right about most things, and she was dead on the mark about that. Bruce and I have hunted and fished and traveled together all over the country.

When I accepted my first teaching job at BV, Bruce was going to school there. He was a junior, and I coached him for two years in football. He was a natural athlete and a pleasure to coach. He went to American River Junior College for two years, then on to the University of Arizona on a full football scholarship. One of his finer moments came against Ohio State in Columbus. He ran a bootleg (on his own) and the touchdown he made won the game. You were NOT supposed to beat Ohio State and Woody at their place.

When my dad got sick with ALS (Lou Gehrig's Disease), Bruce was a huge help for Ma. He was always looking for some way to help out. He continues to do the same thing for us (Ralphene and me) now that my Parkinson's has gotten worse. It would be hard to find a better brother.

He has so many friends, I don't even think he knows them all. He is one fine brother, and I love him.

My Daughter

Susie came into this world a happy smiling child. I could not hold her the first time I saw her at the hospital because I came from a baseball game, and I had poison oak. She has been the grandest daughter. You often hear parents complain about having this problem or that problem with their kids throughout their growing up, but we never did have any of those problems with Suz.

Suz was always self-motivated. I think she inherited that gene and the kind and caring gene from her mother. I remember the time when she was a couple years old when we used to take her to my mother's house to be cared for. She was looking out a front-room window and put her hand on the window. My mother gently admonished her by saying, "Susie, we don't do that because it may make the window look dirty and make more work for Grandma." That was all it took. She never again did anything that would cause her grandma to do extra work. My mother was an immaculate housekeeper. I think she took that gene with her to Heaven.

When Susie was about seven, and David was four, I started taking David to wrestling tournaments on weekends. As his skill grew, we spent more and more weekends at tournaments all over the country. Suz went on almost all of these trips, and was David's Number One Supporter, and never complained. I can still see the two of them riding in the special-spot in the VW camper, which was their small area in the rear of the VW. They played games and entertained themselves for hours on end, never asking, "When are we going to be there?" That special-spot turned into a different special-spot in a bigger camper on our pickup truck. It had a window you could look out going down the road. At that time no seat belts were necessary. Just pure fun.

I fondly remember our first of many trips to Dillon Beach. I can still see Suz on the dock, pulling up crab nets. At that time the crabs were plentiful. We carried bucketfuls back to our camper in the sand dunes where we boiled them in a ten-gallon drum, then sat at the picnic table cleaning them. I can remember bringing back two full "Wonder Bread bags" of pure crab meat. Those years didn't last long, but I will remember them forever.

As a young girl, Susie competed in all sports—softball, volleyball, basketball, and track and was far above average in each one. When she was ready for high school, the San Juan District boundary lines dictated that she attend La Sierra. Because I was teaching at Bella Vista, she could receive a waiver and attend BV. I was not all that sure that she wanted to do that—being at the same school where her father taught. However, the BV coaching staff, all our good friends, urged her to come to BV, which she decided to do. This, as it turned out, did not displease the women's athletic department.

Also, I told her if she got straight As throughout her high school career, when she was ready for college, I would buy her a car of her choice, never really thinking this would be possible. She had an outstanding athletic and academic career at Bella Vista, and graduated with a 4.0. This was in the day before honors classes weighted grades, so this meant As in every course she took. She applied to Stanford and also to UC Davis, not really thinking she had a chance to get into Stanford. Someone had told her that when she received the letter from Stanford, if it was a thick envelope, that was good news. A thin envelope meant you were turned down. The way she received the news is kind of interesting. Ralphene, David, and I were out of town for the weekend at a wrestling tournament. The mail came on Saturday, the first weekend in April, and there was the Stanford envelope. Suz waited until she had us on the phone before opening the letter. We could tell by her screams of joy that

Family

the news was good. We all knew how difficult it was to be admitted to Stanford, and she was excited to be among the chosen few. Now all Ralphene and I had to do was come up with the money for tuition!

Now as to the car—I knew that whatever she chose, I was going to come up with it. However, Susan, being her mother's daughter, allowed me to get off the hook for a used Chevy Chevette bought from Ernie Caddel, who put new tires and new brakes on for free. Cost was $1,300. She appreciated the fact that the Stanford education was going to be very expensive, and she did not want to add to that burden. Bless her!!

She graduated from Stanford with honors and accepted a job in Washington, D.C. with the General Accounting Office. Her mother rode back to D.C. with her in her well-worn car to start her first real job.

I have never had a reason not to be proud of her. She is one very special daughter. More to follow.

Charlie and Susie getting ready for a day in the drift boat on the Madison River in Ennis, Montana, 1997 family vacation at the Power House.

One of a Kind

That term is thrown about a lot where wives are concerned, by their husbands, and I'm sure that they mean it (in most cases).

Ralphene has accomplished so much on her own and been an inspiring influence in so many lives. And yet, still is such a wonderful wife, mother, and grandmother. As a young girl she was a straight 4 point in high school (before you could be 4.7 or whatever). Her success in the horse show ring was unmatched in all the state of Iowa. A Phi Beta Kappa in college, she was a marvelous student. When I left the Houston Oilers and came back to Mt. Pleasant with no job, and too late in the year to get one, not one complaint from her.

We went to Central Missouri State College where I obtained my master's degree, and she went to work at Whiteman Air Force Base as a kindergarten teacher for $2,800 a year. We were so poor I used to hustle local high school kids for a dime a game in pool. Never a complaint from her.

Ralphene was an only child and dearly loved her folks, but when I took a job in California, no complaints, though I knew she wanted to be closer to home.

She enjoyed my love of coaching football, and she understood the game. When it came to wrestling, she didn't know a stand-up from a takedown. And contrary to football, I was gone most Saturdays. No complaints. Instead, she learned how to keep score and how to organize tournaments.

In the summer months, even before Suz and David were born, I used to go to freestyle tournaments with my high school wrestlers. Along she would come, finally learning the complexities of freestyle scoring and pairing. She was never too proud to ask questions. Eventually she became one of the few FILA Pairing Masters Exceptionelle in the USA. She was chosen by USA Wrestling to be the U.S. pairing master to accompany the Olympic team to Barcelona in 1992. All the while being recognized as a California Teacher of the Year in 1997, AND being the only woman thus far to be inducted into the California Wrestling Hall of Fame.

Ralphene—shown here at the Awards Banquet for the Concord International Greco-Roman Wrestling Tournament, a tournament which she helped organize for many years.

She is the person responsible for the Sacramento Super Stars. The whole thing was her idea. I just thought it sounded pretty good and went from there. But the concept was hers. And she did a wonderful behind-the-scenes job working with the parents of that club, which was not an easy task, believe me.

Seeing how hard she worked to become a speaker on education, and develop her programs, yet not for an instant neglect me or the kids, was really something. If one of the kids called, and they needed this or that, she was right there. No complaints. I don't know how many times she flew back to D.C. at the drop of a hat to help Suz out with one thing or another. Never a hint of discontent. When Andy got leukemia, she made a few quick lesson plans and was on the next plane. Gone for four months. Not one complaint.

Only I know what she has been and is going through with me with this Parkinson's. Just keeping track of the meds would be a full-time job for most people. But doing that on top of the everyday things like keeping house, shopping, doing most of the cooking, putting up with my getting up at one or two in the morning and stomping around the house. Not one time showing irritation. Never showing any frustration when I went through those awful vomiting spells and terrible bouts of depression. And now, with this speech thing, she never gets impatient or irritated with me, especially when I write these e-mails and am constantly asking how to spell a word or punctuate a phrase. She has put up with a lot in 44 years. I owe a debt I can never repay.

Paint Job

I decided to paint the house one summer. Yellow seemed a good choice. I thought that spray painting would be best, but my dad swore by hand painting with an old-fashioned brush. So hand painting it was. It was slow work; I was not the best painter. One day I had just opened a brand-new gallon can of yellow paint. I climbed up the ladder and set the can on the top shelf, when I slipped and fell straight backwards, the whole can of paint landing on me, making for one funny sight (or at least Ralphene thought so).

Black or White

One fall day Ralphene decided it was time to enclose the patio in plastic to prevent the rain from getting in. We did this every year before rainy season, and I always hated doing it and would leave some of the screen at the top free of the plastic because it was hard to reach. Ralphene had gone someplace, and this year I decided to do the job right. I enclosed every inch of the screen in plastic. I did my best job ever and was so proud of it—I just couldn't wait for her to see it. When she got home, she walked out in the kitchen and let out an awful yell. I came running, "What's the trouble?" I yelled. "You used black plastic!" she says. "So what?" I replied, "I got it for half the price of clear!" Well, nothing would calm her down until I had taken down the black and replaced it with clear. You never know what a woman thinks!!!!!!!!!!!

The Lemon Tree

I always enjoyed trying to do little things to make Ralphene happy. This one didn't go so well. We had a lovely lemon tree in our back yard, and Ralphene would make lemon pies and lemon bars, and she loved to give lemons to our friends.

Well, one afternoon when I knew she was gone for a while, I had a plan I thought was brilliant. I went to my mom's and borrowed her electric juicer, and I stopped and bought a bag full of plastic ice cube trays. I was set!

I got the ladder and picked the lemons from the tree—yes, all of them. I halved them and juiced them and put the juice in the ice cube trays to put in the freezer so my honey would have lemon juice any time she needed it! Well, when Ralphene walked in, the first thing she saw was a huge sticky mess. I hadn't quite finished cleaning up. Then when she saw what I had done—to help!—I was in big trouble! I guess I missed the concept of having those FRESH lemons available anytime she wanted them! (This was just a few months after the black plastic episode, so I was in double trouble.)

Be Careful What You Say

We had gone to Slocum House Restaurant in Fair Oaks for dinner. Our waiter was very efficient and conscientious. I told him, "You're doing a great job. I'm giving you a 10!" That really seemed to please him. Ralphene said, "You know what you just did, don't you?" "What?" "Now he thinks you are going to tip him $10!" Well, that was the furthest thing from my mind. I just meant on a scale of 1 to 10, I would give his service a 10. Naturally I ended up tipping him $10. You have to be careful what you say!

Travel Update

Had an uneventful trip back to Maryland. We took our usual Highway 80 route. Good weather, took six days, which is normal, although I used to do it in three. Stopped in Des Moines so Ralphene could get her Maid-Rite hamburger fix for the year. We met her best friend Sonja and Sone's husband Lefty (a retired school superintendent) for breakfast. They live in Clarion, about a two-hour drive north on Highway 95. That's always the highlight of the trip for Ralphene, and she makes breakfast last until lunch. Sonja makes the world's best toffee, and I could sit and listen to Lefty for hours, so I don't mind. We are now enjoying the grandkids.

Basketball season is just getting underway, so we are gearing up for lots of bleacher time and filming. I go with a fishing guide on Monday to the Shenandoah National Forest for some brook trout fishing. Just got a new rod (took two years to have it especially made by a rod maker in New York, just for me) so am anxious to give it a test. I thought in the years we have been coming here, that we had eaten in every restaurant in the D.C. area, but Ralphene keeps coming up with new ones. Am taking a brief rest now.

Johnny Cash
By Ralphene

My friends know that I am quite a concertgoer. It hasn't always been that way though. In fact, I recall the very first big-time concert that I attended. Charlie and I were big Johnny Cash fans back in the day. I heard that he was coming to Oakland Coliseum (this was in May of 1971) and we decided to get a group of our friends from Bella Vista together and attend the concert. First we planned dinner at The Elegant Farmer in Jack London Square—a favorite restaurant of the BV crew.

The concert happened to fall on our daughter Susie's seventh birthday, so Charlie had the bright idea of giving Suz a choice of having a birthday party for her friends or going to Johnny Cash with us. You can guess which one she chose! What an education for her! We were right behind a large group of Hell's Angels! Susie had a few questions about them, I remember.

During the concert, I recall Johnny Cash looking over at someone standing against a side wall and saying, "Hey, Joplin—get on up here!" And yes, it was Janis Joplin! The two of them did several songs together. How awesome was that! So that is the story of my first concert and my daughter's rather memorable seventh birthday.

Shopping with the Rich and Famous
By Ralphene

One Christmas Charlie and I were back in Maryland—the grandkids would have been about two, four, and six. It was Christmas Eve Day, and we all decided it would be fun to go to

Union Station in downtown D.C. Union Station is an experience in itself, and at Christmastime it has this fabulous model train set up in the center of the building. (Matt was at the age when he LOVED model trains. Andy always has!)

We all rode the Metro downtown, and we spent a lot of time eating, poking around the shops, just enjoying ourselves. We had been there a couple hours. It was evening by now, and a voice came over the loudspeaker requesting that everyone move to the upper level of the mall. We grown-ups quickly looked around and grabbed the three kids by the hands. We moved upstairs and stood at the railing to see what the heck was going on. We count heads and no one sees Charlie. But we aren't worried about him. He is on his scooter, and he has a habit of disappearing quite frequently! Now we see the Secret Service detail come through the double doors. Followed by—President Clinton! The President had decided to come over and do his Christmas shopping—on Christmas Eve! So in he comes; you could have heard a pin drop. Just Clinton and his security guys. The first store he goes into is Brookstone. Well, Susie and I were standing there together, looking across the mall and down into that store, and we both noticed the same thing. At the back of the store is a figure on a red scooter—guess who!! So Charlie and President Clinton were the only people shopping in Brookstone! How many guys could pull that one off?

Rolling in $

Before leaving Maryland to return to California one year after a six-month stay in Rockville, I wanted to give the Special Three one last fun thing to remember. I took 100 one-dollar bills to Susie's and spread them all over the backyard. There is a large hill in the backyard, and I put them over the whole area.

The rules were these. You had to start at the top of the hill, with one arm tied to your side. Each kid had a container at the top of the hill. On my command they would race down the hill and grab no more than two dollar bills, return to the top of the hill and place them in their jar. Then make another trip. The kids thought this was great fun, of course, but after a few trips up and down the hill, they were pooped. Of course they did not want a sibling to get more money than they had, so they pushed on. When it was all over, the kids were dragging, but surprisingly, they were within a couple of dollars of having the same amount of money. Lots of fun!!!

South of the Border

This is quite a story. And since it involves wrestling, I'll tell it. In 1980 David made the World Schoolboy Wrestling Team. The world tournament was to be held in Mexico City. The AAU Grand Nationals, the qualifying tournament, had been held in Lincoln, Nebraska. David had spent the two weeks preceding the tourney in Oregon at Marc Sprague's USA Oregon training camp. Ralphene, Susie, and I were in Mt. Pleasant for part of the summer, and we all met up in Lincoln. David had quite a tournament there (this is where he beat Blake Bonjean). After the qualifying tournament, the team was to spend a week training in Lincoln before flying to Mexico City. So Ralphene, Susie, and I returned to Mt. Pleasant to enjoy more time in Iowa with Ralphene's mom. I fished the local farm ponds and played golf everyday with A. Lloyd Spooner (Ralphene's uncle). After three days of that, I asked Ralphene if she would like to go for a ride. "Sure," she said, "where?" "Mexico City," says I. So off we go. Susie stayed with her grandmother for a few more days, then came home on the train. She said it was her best summer yet. Had we known what lay ahead over the next 3,400 miles we traveled in Mexico, I suppose we would have gone anyway. But what a trip!

When we got to the U.S./Mexico border we were told we had to have travel insurance. $225. We got in a very long line. A shady-looking character came up to me and asked if I would like to not have to wait in such a long line. I replied, "No thanks." Another 30 minutes passed, and we hadn't moved. The guy approached me again. Well, you don't have to hit me on the head with a two by four to see what's happening. I followed him into a little room. I departed $25 poorer, but we were soon in Mexico and on our way. (We later realized that the waiting line was made up of locals who were paid a few pesos each day to stand in that line! No wonder it never moved!) At our first gas stop we were surrounded by a group of eight to ten young boys (maybe 11 or 12 years old) who wanted to be helpful by washing our windshield and even pumping the gas. I caught the scam just in time. They would put in the gas without resetting the pump, buyer beware!! This little game was to repeat itself many times while in Mexico. The countryside was pretty barren—a small village here and there, off in the distance. We took a couple of side roads to see what country life was like. Real poverty. No wonder the people wanted to come to the USA. We went incredibly-long distances without seeing another town or car. It was always a concern that we would run out of gas or break down. The Mexican government provided service in the form of green trucks (I called them repair shops on wheels) that would come along now and then to give aid if needed.

It was very hot, and the first time we stopped for a bite to eat, I ordered a Coke. (It seemed Coke was the national drink.) I had to drink it warm. No refrigeration. This was common in the countryside. When we arrived in Mexico City we checked into the hotel where the U.S. team was staying and parked our station wagon in the underground parking area. We were never to move it until we left seven days later. The hotel was nice enough. It was in what was known as the "Zona Rosa," the Pink Zone. I was anxious to try some REAL Mexican food. There was a buffet at the hotel so we tried it, and found it outstanding in every respect. That was the last good meal we had until McDonald's in the U.S.

I was determined to get some real Mexican cooking. So against the advice of our liaison leader, Oswaldo Smith, I headed for old-town Mexico City. It turned out that we were both right. I got some really delicious tacos and chicken mole. Also Montezuma's Revenge! Ralphene showed me no pity.

The tournament was held at a local high school. We arrived early. We always rode with the team on the team bus. It was an old broken-down orange bus driven by a man named Hector. He knew only one mode—FULL SPEED AHEAD and lean on the horn. Some of those rides would have put the Disneyland rides to shame. As I said, we arrived at the tournament site early, and there were no mats in sight yet. We waited and waited—no mats. There were not as many teams entered as originally thought, and the tournament was to last five days. The Mexican Wrestling Association had just the answer—one mat.

The tournament dragged on forever. The nice part of this was that the families got to know each other very well. Lanny Bryant and I took the team to a bullfight, and Ralphene and Ann Bryant countered with the Ballet Folklorico for everyone. This actually turned out to be a great outing! I kept looking for that perfect meal. One day I wanted to find a travel agency to cash in the return leg of David's ticket, since he would ride home with us. I hailed a taxi and told the driver the name of the place I wanted to go. It was like a comedy skit. He drove me around the block and let me off at a place not 100 yards from the hotel—$5 please.

The Mexican police had the best scam. There were two officers dressed absolutely immaculately, not a crease out of place, the dark glasses, shiny motorcycle boots, the gloves, everything just perfect. They would park their cycles about 25 yards down the street from the front steps of the hotel. One of them would stay with the bikes while the other would come stand on the third step of the hotel. This gave him just the height he needed to be seen and heard above the traffic. The best way I know to describe the Mexico City traffic would be to liken it to a beehive run amuck. In front of our hotel, four, or maybe even five traffic lanes came together. Horns blaring, Mexicans of all shapes and sizes running up to a car when it stopped for a red light, wanting to wash your window for whatever you might give them. And here stands the cop, looking cool and calm, amidst all the hubbub and roar. He casts a smile you could see for a mile—before he drops the hammer.

He would blow his whistle and slightly motion with one perfectly-gloved finger at some poor cab driver. The cab driver would pull over (never once did they not pull over). The ever-vigilant protector of the peace would proceed to the cab, ever so softly place his right foot on the bumper and pull out his note pad. I know not what was said, but in each and every case the cabby would pull the calfskin, or in some cases, if he had a passenger, the passenger would pull his. And this same scene would be repeated until this one officer of the law needed a break. Then his partner would take over. I asked Oswaldo about this, and he said, "Oh, yes, this is very common." It looked to me like a good way to add to the monthly bottom line. I understand there is no such thing as a welfare check in Mexico, so it's every man for himself.

Family

When the tournament was finally over, (David pinned all his opponents) and we were set to check out of the hotel, I asked for our bill. It was like $1,600!! I couldn't believe it. We went once again to Oswaldo and said we only had about $300 on us. This must be a mistake. Well, after much hollering and gesturing, the thing was settled.

As soon as we crossed the border at Tijuana, we made a beeline for the Golden Arches. The USA never looked so good to us!

Parkinson's Disease

I was first diagnosed with Parkinson's disease in 1992. I was still teaching at Bella Vista. I had always planned on retiring at age 55, and this news just settled the matter for me. I think it was some time in 1990 or 1991 that I noticed a sort of numbness in my left hand when I shaved. I also had more trouble moving my left foot compared to my right. I paid little attention to those things, as neither was painful or limited me from doing anything I wanted to do.

About two years after I retired in 1994, the symptoms started to get a little worse. I began to have trouble with coordination in my left hand. I could not stack poker chips (that's when I first noticed it). My left hand would also shake, and I had no control over this. This stage lasted about six months, during which time I also started to have a hard time walking. I would freeze—be unable to move. By now it was almost impossible to turn over in bed at night.

That condition continues to this day. Regarding the freezing, we found that by putting something on the floor in front of me, I could step over it and thus start walking again. Ralphene would carry throw pillows in the van just in case I froze and could not make it to the front door, which happened very frequently. One evening we went to dinner at the Broiler Restaurant in downtown Sacramento. When it came time to leave, I could not walk. Ralphene took some linen napkins off the tables and dropped them on the floor about 18 inches apart. I proceeded to step over them, and we made it out of the restaurant. That condition lasted about two years and was a bit of a problem, because when my meds were working, I could do pretty much what I wanted. I could usually tell when the pills were wearing off, and sometimes by taking additional meds, I could avoid the problems. But not always. Many was the time I would be at the Phoenix or Lucky Derby Card Club, and not be able to get up and leave. Sometimes I would get to the men's room and not be able to get my pants up after using the toilet. But most of the time, if you were to run into me on the street, you would never know anything was wrong.

That condition lasted probably a year and a half. Then it started to get much worse. I thought I was going to be home-bound. The thought of being able to walk a stream and actually fly fish was just a dream, I feared. During this entire five or six-year period we continued to see the doctors and constantly change/adjust medications. We also began driving to Washington, D.C. to be near our grandkids. We rented an apartment very near the Stadniks so the kids could walk over anytime they wanted. It was about the year 2000 that I also began to have speech problems. My inability to walk was becoming serious, and I started to have periods of severe depression. Before this, I could never understand why some people would have nervous breakdowns or say they were so depressed that nothing seemed to matter. I also started throwing up in the evenings, usually around 8 or 9 pm. This was hard on Ralphene. At night I thought I would never be able to get through the next day. And I did not look forward to anything. We were planning a trip that summer to Colorado to a dude ranch for a week with the whole family, plus our dear friends Barry Alan and Linda Winthers. When those depression moods hit, I had absolutely no desire to go, and I thought I would not be able to make it. We began to fool around with my medications (Ralphene deserves all the credit here) and lo and behold, the doctor came up with a combination that virtually eliminated the freezing and also did away with the vomiting and the depression.

It was like getting a new lease on life. My speech got worse, but at least I could walk fairly well. I did not have to worry about freezing while at a basketball game or restaurant. We made the summer trip to Colorado, and it felt like being in Heaven to be able to get on the Colorado River and fly fish. I could not walk too far and would need help getting out of the water, so Bruce would lend me his arm. It seemed awful good to me!

I have a lot of pain in my shoulders, hips, elbows, neck, and all over. The doctors say it is partly Parkinson's related and partly

Family

arthritis. I have been on all sorts of meds. We tried acupuncture for several weeks while in Maryland, but no good. But this is manageable. After a while, it just becomes part of your life. The uncontrolled shaking of my hand has disappeared. The freezing occurs rarely. The depression is mostly gone. It would come on at night and in the morning be gone. Strange.

Right now I would say I have had Parkinson's for 15 years. I feel I have been lucky. I have seen what it has done to some people. It affects people in such different ways. I am frustrated that I can not speak clearly. The grandkids can understand me pretty much, so that is most important. I am able to go fly fishing once in a while, with Ralphene's help. Right now I feel best around ten or eleven in the morning. At this time I have taken two doses of meds, plus two percoset. The neurologist had me on morphine tablets, 4-6 a day, but they did no better than the percoset. I am able to function pretty well until around 7 or 8 at night. Then I start to stiffen up, and by bedtime I am hurting pretty good. I have been on Ambien for sleep for almost three years. You could say I am addicted. I don't sleep too well. I am up three or four times a night to pee, and then am up for good at 5:30. Read the paper, play on-line chess, watch the news, and try to do this without disturbing Ralphene. That has been the pattern since we arrived in October. We are still working on the meds. I will not complain if things stay as they are. Being able to drive and go fishing once in a while and watch the kids' games, and life is good.

While on vacation with the family in Maryland over the Christmas holidays, I woke up one morning and could not urinate. I was starting to hurt, and Ralphene called the advice nurse at Kaiser Hospital in Washington, D.C. We were about two hours away, but the nurse said to go to the closest emergency room. We ended up going to a hospital in Easton, Maryland—15 minutes from where we were staying. I have never felt such pain. They put a catheter in me and drained 1,500 cc of urine. That was the greatest feeling I think I ever had. We left the catheter in, attached to a bag on my leg. When we got back to D.C. I called Kaiser, and they said to leave it in for seven days, then come in and see the urologist. After seven days I went in. I saw a nurse who removed the catheter and put 200 cc of water into me. Now I was to see if I could urinate on my own. I went about 100 cc. The nurse said to drink 24 ounces of water and walk around for 30 minutes and see if I could pee. I did this and peed about another 100 cc. They thought I would be ok and sent me home. The next morning I was stopped up again and was in even more pain than before. I did not think that possible. Ralphene drove me to the urologist's office at Kaiser. We went in and told the receptionist I needed to be seen right away. That was at 8:20 am. I was ready to tear the place apart, I was in such pain. I was getting desperate. At 9:05 they got me in, and a nurse gave me another catheterization. Again I felt like a new person. This time the urologist came in and told me to wear the catheter and leg bag for another week and come back and see how things were going. If I was no better, the nurse would show me how to do self-catheterization. Seven days later I am back again. The nurse removes the catheter, and I do the water routine again. Just to be on the safe side, she shows me how to do the catheterization myself. We go home and over the next week I use the catheter probably two dozen times. Ralphene has to help me most of those times. Then, all of a sudden, for the last two weeks I have been able to go on my own. I am keeping my fingers crossed that this will last.

Charlie and Ralphene at a stop in Des Moines on their trip east to Maryland in 2004. (Thank you, Sone!)

Family

I would not be able to live on my own. No possible way. The type of caregiver is crucial when dealing with Parkinson's. And I have the absolute best. Ralphene does it all. She takes care of all my meds—ordering them when I need them, organizing them, and seeing to it I take them on time. That is just a HUGE job. She helps me get out of a chair, whether it is at home or out in public, and always gives me a kiss when I am up. She never loses her temper or patience, and I am not always the easiest person to live with. She takes care of all doctors' appointments, does all the grocery shopping, washes all the clothes, plus Sam's, helps Sam every night with her homework, does most of the cooking. And she does all of this with a positive attitude. I could not begin to get along without her. I would just have to go to a nursing home.

I feel sorry for those people with any debilitating disease who do not have a good caregiver. I believe it is harder on the caregiver than the person with the disorder. Right now we are taking it one day at a time. I hope we will be able to drive home again this June and have one more family get-together this summer.

Humpty-Dumpty

Since I met up with Mr. Parkinson, I have taken some memorable falls. I am describing them only because in looking back at them, I can laugh at myself because I was fortunate not to have gotten seriously hurt.

Fall One: I was cleaning our fish pond. And standing on the third level of rock which was roughly four feet above the pond surface. Somehow I managed to slip and fall over backward, flat on my back in the pond. Now this pond is constructed of jagged lava rock. I was lucky—I only got wet.

Fall Two: We were shopping at the Ikea Store in West Sacramento. Ralphene was checking out at the counter, and I was waiting patiently on my scooter. I said, "I'll meet you at the car." She replied, "Stay put and have some patience. I'll be done soon." I said, "I'll be OK, don't worry, I'll be careful," and I motored off to our car. I broke the scooter down into four parts and began to put them in the trunk of the Cadillac. As I was putting the last piece in, I lost my balance and fell flat on my back on the hot asphalt. About that time, Ralphene came around the corner to see me down, and half a dozen people wanting to do everything from helping me up, to calling 911, to calling an ambulance. I thought I had broken something, but it turned out I just took a good fall and was quite stiff for a few days.

Fall Three: We were on vacation with the whole clan at the ocean. We had just returned from an outing at the Santa Cruz Boardwalk. Everyone else had gone inside, and I decided I wanted to ride around on my scooter and take in some scenery. As I rode the scooter backwards out of the van, the back somehow caught on something, and I went straight over backward with the scooter landing flat on top of me. I thought for sure I was gonna be badly hurt as I started to go over. Lucky again—just a little shook up.

Fall Four: I was having a yard sale and was tacking up a cardboard sign across the street on a street pole. Don't know what happened, but next thing I knew, I was falling and about to land on some very scary-looking cactus. I had the presence of mind to kind of lunge and landed on some grass and brick instead. Hurt some, but no real damage.

Fall Five: I was at my brother's house by myself. I had just raided his fridge and gone into the great room to watch TV. I sat down a little too fast and too hard, and his rocker/recliner went straight over backwards. I landed on my back, wedged between his fireplace and a table, with my legs in the air and the rocker on top of me. I felt like a turtle! It took a good 20 minutes to get free.

There have been many other falls, but these come to mind simply because they are the type of falls that my wife and daughter laugh at. (Some sense of humor.)

Old Age and Other Blessings

I can remember when my father turned 70. I thought he was old. My aunts and five uncles were in their early 80s when they passed away, and despite having relatively good health, seldom left the house, and for their last ten or so years, complained about everything.

My grandfather was 71 and on a train trip to Arizona when an embolism felled him at the train station in Los Angeles. He, however, lived every day as if it were his last. Quite a contrast.

I was at my father's bedside when he passed away after a five-year battle with ALS. I only hope I can show the same attitude and grace that he did when my time comes. My wife is almost 70, yet she seems to be the same person that I married almost 50 years ago. Her energy has hardly slowed. Considering she has been married to me for that time probably qualifies her for Sainthood.

As for myself, as I write this I am five months shy of 70. I have been forced to give up driving. When I look in the mirror, I see a lack of muscle tone. I take enough pills to keep a pharmaceutical company in the black, and most of my friends share these same traits. When I was in my teens, 60 was the age that I considered to be old. I thought that I would have had a pretty good life if I could live that long.

My advice to any young person who says they dread getting to 60: I would say—hope that you are healthy. Having lived with Parkinson's for the past 15 years, I have learned to really appreciate life. I am still able to fish, an activity I have pursued since my early years, not nearly to the same extent, but at a level that lets me appreciate it all the more. I am able to get out and go most anyplace I choose, with a little help from others.

Having spent two weeks in the hospital a few years ago, thinking I had cancer or some other fatal illness, I really appreciate what I have. I have a wife who is truly special. I don't need to go into what makes her special. Those who know her know what I mean. The activities that I am able to do on a day-to-day basis are directly due to her care (what a lucky man). Someone once said that old age is a state of mind. I would wholeheartedly agree.

I look forward to each and every day. My days go something like this. I awaken about 3 or 4 am, watch the news, (ask Ralphene if the TV is too loud) or play on-line chess. Ralphene and I usually talk about going to a movie or where to have lunch or give our grandkids a call. Should we take our beloved Nala to Doggie Park? Or we may drive out to see my brother, Bruce. We are truly blessed to have Bruce nearby. We are also lucky to have David close by. He has been with us many days for the past few months. I have been able to have anything I want for breakfast, lunch, or dinner. It's amazing what a mother will do for her son that she won't do for her husband of 49 years. If I desire any particular dish, I just tell David, and we have it.

I am always looking forward to some fishing trip I have planned. It has taken a while, but I have really come to appreciate the things I <u>can</u> do, rather than what I can't. It is surprising how many things a person can do if he will learn to put up with a little pain. It is not all that hard. As I see old age, the only drawback, and it is a big one, is having to rely on others. Do all that you can for yourself and appreciate what others do for you.

In a nut shell: For me, what I truly enjoy is going to bed knowing the next morning I will be able to do just what I want to do.

Family

*Bella Vista coaches Gordon Pistochini, Charlie Lee, Don Driscoll,
and Larry Fletcher at the 1999 wedding of Don's daughter, Mary.*

In Memoriam

On September 9, 2010, Charles O. Lee, Jr. passed away peacefully at his home in Carmichael, California, after living with Parkinson's disease for over twenty years. Charlie was 71 years old. A Memorial Service was held on December 28, 2010 in the Bella Vista High School gymnasium. A crowd of several hundred people filled the bleachers on one side of the gym that evening. Large posters of Charlie's life were on easels throughout the gym, and the Bella Vista wrestling mat was placed in the center of the gym floor, mat lamp above it, as it had been for so many of Bella Vista's home matches.

The Lee family at the December 2010 Memorial Service for Charlie.

Article taken from *The University of Iowa College of Education Alumni Magazine,* **Spring 2013.**

Remembering **Charles Lee**

Charles Lee

Charles O. Lee (BA '61) was a great coach, a great teacher, and a great Hawkeye. Throughout his life, he exemplified the importance of education, athletic fundamentals, and the value of hard work.

Lee was a tackle on the Hawkeye football team from 1958 to 1961. He was a three-time letter winner and contributed to a national title, two Rose Bowl championships, and three Big Ten Championships. After a brief stint in professional football, Lee spent 32 years as a physical education teacher and football and wrestling coach at Bella Vista High School in Fair Oaks, Calif.

Because he saw a need for young wrestlers in his community to have a place to practice their sport, Lee formed the Sacramento Superstars, a kids' wrestling program that he coached to three national team championships.

Lee was named the Scholastic Wrestling News National Coach of the Year in 1979 and inducted into the California Wrestling Hall of Fame in 2001, thanks in part to his school's incredible 242-28-1 overall dual meet record. Lee also had the rare opportunity to coach his son, David, a three-time high school wrestling state champion in California.

Friends of Lee, who died after a 20-year battle with Parkinson's disease on Sept. 9, 2010, say even those high honors don't adequately capture the impact Lee had on others throughout his life.

"Charlie demonstrated a remarkable ability to build networks, to touch people's hearts, to inspire giving, and to lead," says his friend and fellow Hawkeye football alumnus, William Ringer (BBA '63). "He believed deeply in the power of goodwill and integrity and dedicated his life to bringing those two forces together in order to better the people around him."

When Lee passed away, his wife Ralphene received more than 165 emails from athletes and students whom he had influenced over the

This *Young Wrestler* magazine cover illustrates Lee's relationship with his nine-year-old son, David, who is also in the California Wrestling Hall of Fame.

years. One came from Scott Smith, a special agent in the Federal Bureau of Investigation, who credits Coach Lee with helping him transform from "an overweight kid with a bad attitude," to a successful adult.

"I always knew that Coach Lee was interested in seeing me be the best I could be both as an athlete and a person," Smith wrote. "He changed my life; there is no doubt about it. I believe if he had not been interested in my success, I would have continued down an unfortunate path."

Ralphene Lee (BA '61) says her husband always enjoyed being around young people and helping them be their best.

"I really can't explain it. He was the type of guy who was there for the kids. It was just part of him," Ralphene says. "And it wasn't just the athletes. Charlie was there for the underdog kid, or the kid who didn't have as much in the way of athletic talent. He'd take them fishing or out for a hamburger, the ones who needed extra guidance. That's just how he was."

> "Charlie demonstrated a remarkable ability to build networks, to touch people's hearts, to inspire giving, and to lead," says his friend and fellow Hawkeye football alumnus, William Ringer (BBA '63).

The Lees met at the UI and were married during their senior year in a black-and-gold-themed wedding. Ralphene says the wedding happened earlier than they'd planned because Charlie was invited to play in the Hula Bowl in Hawaii and players could take their wives along for free.

"I guess that was pretty good motivation," she says with a laugh. "We had quite a time at the UI."

Ralphene also enjoyed a long, successful career in education. She taught elementary school for 30 years and was named the California Teacher of the Year in 1997. She is also the only woman to have been inducted to the California Wrestling Hall of Fame because of her involvement as a pairing master. Her work behind the scenes in wrestling spanned everything from small, local tournaments to traveling to Barcelona with the U.S. Olympic team in 1992.

"When you're married to a coach, you're either totally involved or you don't have anything to do with it," Ralphene says. "I was the type that was totally involved in everything

Bella Vista High School squad gives Coach Lee a ride after an important team victory.

Charlie and his wrestlers were doing."

The Lee family's impact in education and wrestling in California and beyond was profound, but their motivation was simple. In a *Sacramento Sports Magazine* article about his coaching accomplishments, Lee described his expectations for his student athletes as "a little corny."

Charles and Ralphene Lee intently watch the wrestlers in action.

"I like the kids to do just a few basic things: come to practice on time, work hard when they're in the room, keep their grades up, use good common sense, and be good citizens," he said. Lee's friend, Ringer, says a famous quote reminds him of the way Lee lived.

"Winston Churchill once quipped, 'We make a living by what we get, but we make a life by what we give.' Charlie followed this principle to a tee," Ringer says. "He devoted his life to helping others and giving unselfishly to those in need."

Four Hawkeye linemen from the 1959 Rose Bowl Championship team were in the Lees' black-and-gold-themed wedding on December 10, 1960, in Mt. Pleasant, Iowa. After the wedding, the couple flew to Houston, Texas, to attend the Bluebonnet Bowl as guests of Bud Adams, owner of the Houston Oilers, with whom Lee later signed.

In Memoriam

Charlie Lee, Don Driscoll, Larry Fletcher, and Gordon Pistochini were later affectionately known by many as "The Four Horsemen." They raised their families together and remained close friends after retirement, participating in a weekly very competitive cribbage game.

Targe Lindsay, Bella Vista principal from 1975-1983, was Master of Ceremonies for Charlie's Memorial Service.

Larry Fletcher, football and track coach at Bella Vista for many years.

Targe Lindsay, Bruce Summers (Charlie's assistant wrestling coach), and Gordon Pistochini enjoying Larry's jokes.

Tim Driscoll, son of football coach Don Driscoll.

Gordon Pistochini coached basketball and football at Bella Vista for many years.

Mike Lee, Bella Vista wrestling coach since 1994.

The Lee family at the Power House in Ennis, Montana in 1997.

To view a 10-minute slideshow of Charlie's life presented at his memorial service, please visit Ralphene's YouTube channel at:

www.youtube.com/user/ralphenelee

ON IOWA